# What Will Set You Free

## From Pain to Passion
### in 7 Weeks

*by*

*Cynthia James*

Cover Art
by Doug Haverty of Art & Soul

Photography
by Carl Studna


Meditation CD:
All Rights Reserved
Copyright 2007 by Cynthia James

Piano Synthesizer: Kent Rautenstraus
Mix Engineer: Park Peters
Mixed & Mastered: Audio Park Studios


Book:
A Books To Believe In Publication
All Rights Reserved
Copyright 2007 by Cynthia James

Proudly Published in the USA by
Thornton Publishing, Inc
17011 Lincoln Ave. #408
Parker, CO 80134
www.ProfitablePublishing.net
Phone: 303.794.8888
Fax:   720.863.2013



www.WhatWillSetYouFree.com
www.BooksToBelieveIn.com/Freedom.php


ISBN: 0-9774761-8-9

# THIS BOOK BELONGS TO THE AMAZING:

_____

# GRAFFITI KOAN

Daniel Roth

Roaring down I-95
thirteen or fourteen summers ago
van full of boxes bags
and apprehension
new wife
my thirteen-year-old daughter
who would lose her way
due to my own neglect
start a new life
in San Francisco

speeding through the derelict streets
of Connecticut
old abandoned mills
life gone by
then I see it
across a footbridge
between the projects
shaky graffiti scrawl
not flowing tattoo-like swirls
this guy must have hung from a fence
cars flying by at seventy miles an hour
and I see his words:

## WHAT WILL SET YOU FREE?

**reprinted with permission from the author from his book**
**ORDINARY LIFE: IN THREE ACTS**

This book
is dedicated to
my mother, Susan,
and the generations
of family members who
have struggled to
express their
divinity.

# ACKNOWLEDGEMENTS

"Brilliant! This is inspired writing. Given the sensitivity of the questions and issues people will bring to the book, it is completely respectful. People can identify with the case studies and see themselves in the stories. The exercises are profound. Anyone who seriously wants to intervene in patterns of thinking they have in their life will find this to be a remarkable way to come to high ground, find new understanding and different perspective."

**Barry Heerman**
author of *Noble Purpose*

"Cynthia James has written a compassionate and practical book that speaks to us all with wisdom, clarity, and encouragement about healing emotional wounds of the past and living our life's vision with confidence, creativity and triumph."

**Michael Bernard Beckwith**
Founder and Spiritual Director of
Agape International Spiritual Center,
author of *Inspirations of the Heart*,
*Forty Day Mind Fast*
*Soul Feast*, & *A Manifesto of Peace*

"Cynthia James is a powerful, loving light for healing and wholeness in the world, and her work is reflective of the brilliance of her spirit and the kindness of her heart. I am honored and delighted to recommend her work to anyone seeking a healing of their past so that they might live a free and happy life."

**Katherine Woodward Thomas**
author of *Calling in "The One"*

"After many years of work with victims of child abuse, I can assure you that your message is one that reaches into the hearts and minds of countless adults who have also experienced this pain."

**Deanne Tilton**
Executive Director
Inter-Agency Council on Child Abuse & Neglect
Chairperson, U.S. Advisory Board on Child Abuse & Neglect

# CONTENTS

# FOREWORD

*A human being is like a television set with millions of channels. If we turn the Buddha on, we are the Buddha. If we turn sorrow on, we are sorrow. If we turn a smile on, we really are the smile. We cannot let just one channel dominate us. We have the seed of everything in us, and we have to seize the situation in our hand, to recover our own sovereignty.*

Vietnamese Buddhist author and luminary
Thich Nhat Hanh,
*Being Peace*

If your life has seemed like little more than a relentless soap opera, a painful drama, or an ill-conceived mini-series, take heart. You hold a channel changer in your hands: *What Will Set You Free...From Pain to Passion in 7 Weeks*. This book can help you tune into a new and larger story for your life. It can lead you to true freedom, to recovering your "own sovereignty."

Woundings along the pathway of life are inevitable and nothing to scoff at. The stored up pain is real, searing, and sometimes horrific. These unwanted experiences can seem overpowering and inescapable, as though branded upon mind and heart. Their impact ripples into thoughts and behaviors of the moment and on out into future experiences, often undermining significant relationships and new ventures. Self trust and personal worthiness fade into distant memories. We cry out for a way to heal, a way to restore ourselves to our lost paradise. Yet the overriding tendency is to stay stuck in the vestiges and limiting patterns of a painful past—as though transfixed before our own monotonous and frustrating reruns.

To find authentic healing and true freedom, it is essential to have reliable guidance upon this pathway. You will find this all-important assistance in this compelling book. Cynthia James begins by sharing her own path of healing and empowerment in open, honest and vulnerable ways, thus helping us realize that we are not as alone as once imagined. Then she shares a proven, seven-week program that generates profound insights, healing realizations and visions for an enhanced future. All along the way, Cynthia also provides energizing affirmations, meditations for inner opening, and practices for anchoring and embodying new directions and ways of being.

When I finished my first reading of this book, I realized immediately that this material is so much more than the ordinary collection of self-help adages and feel-good techniques. *What Will Set You Free* is more of a journey-book, an ally for transformation. It takes the explorer into the deep and most confining issues of the past, not merely to grovel some more in the pain and limitation of it all, but to rediscover the potency and creativity of the essential spirit. Then that ember of indestructible spiritual light is fanned into a brilliant flame to illumine a path back to the original beauty and unbounded potential within us all.

I met Cynthia James in 1999 when she provided music and support for a group of us who were facilitating dialogues between His Holiness, The

Dalai Lama, and various researchers, activists, authors, and leaders who were also working for a more enlightened and compassionate future for humankind. From that shared experience, I knew I wanted to continue to work with Cynthia. I was delighted when, in 2004, she agreed to join the ministerial team at Mile Hi Church. She brings to us what she brings to this book: her total authenticity, a personal path of deep and courageous healing, abundant enthusiasm and joy, and an unwavering spiritual consciousness. Before becoming a fine minister, she was an actress and entertainer, moving eventually into various aspects of the business world. With her multitude of talents and perspectives, she is both a marvel and an angel.

This book is so powerful because Cynthia has walked the path herself... and come back to offer us all a route to renewal and freedom. When you have completed her seven-week program, I am confident that you will want to share the opportunity with family and friends-and maybe even an old enemy, or two! You will definitely want to guide yourself through the program numerous times. From my own experience, I know that the healing path is like peeling back the layers of an onion. It's an ever unfolding process. The good news is that, along the way, the tears decrease while the joy and freedom expand.

So delve into this channel changing guidebook. Give yourself the opportunity to surf through untold vistas and programs for your enrichment and liberation. Explore and embrace new and higher frequencies of awareness and livingness. Yes, let this book turn on the avatar or Buddha in you... the compassionate healer in you... the courageous adventurer in you... the open-hearted lover in you… the creative visionary in you… the inspired difference-maker in you… and, moreover, the real and remarkable **YOU** in you!

~Dr. Roger W. Teel
Senior Minister and Spiritual Director
Mile Hi Church
Lakewood, Colorado

# GRATITUDES

*I want to take this opportunity to acknowledge my gratitude to people who have made this project possible.*

Beloved Spirit. There are no words to describe the gratitude I feel for the honor of being a messenger of the divine. I feel honored that I can be a vessel for this message.

My dear mother, a living example of someone who has continued to search for peace and a life filled with love.

To my beloved husband, Carl, your support and unprecedented belief in me consistently reminds me of the blessed life that I live.

My wonderful children, Lee and wife Monique, Sharron, daughter-in-law Shannon. You continue to remind me that I am here to love.

My grandchildren, Brionne, Mycah and Zion. You live in my heart and light up my life. It is my intention to leave a legacy that will make you proud.

My sistah circle: Chemin, Debbie, Eisha, Rene, Tina and Shirley Jo – I love that we have grown up together and that you continue to inspire me in amazing ways.

Teacher and Mentor, Rev. Michael Beckwith. You consistently and constantly exhibit God in action. I am honored to walk this path with you.

Dr. Roger W. Teel and ministerial team of Mile Hi Church. I am so excited to be a part of this amazing ministry. I feel blessed to learn and grow with you.

Lisa Williams, your faith in me was such a support to continue this process.

EJ Thornton, Carol Righthouse, Doug Haverty, Shane DeRolf, Kathy Young, Jean Hendry and my editors. I am so grateful that each of you have shared your talent and wisdom.

Contributing writers to this book. I applaud your authentic sharings. Your stories are inspiring and will assist many in their personal transformations.

My students and clients – you are such gifts to me. Your willingness and courage is an example of grace in action.

# INTRODUCTION

**Definition of Freedom:** The condition of being free of restraints; Liberty of a person from oppression; Exception from unpleasant convictions

Welcome! This definition is why this book could be important to you. Freedom is a choice. It is an opportunity to stand in the full expression of who you are. It is an opportunity to absolutely fulfill the destiny that we have come here to achieve. It is a powerful way of expressing. It is a powerful way of being. It is a way in which we can speak, think, move, and act as amazing human beings. I am so glad that you decided to read this book because what that means to me is that you have decided to take a chance to move beyond the wounds and the feelings that no longer support you.

I feel this book can be important for you because I have always been a seeker. I have always been one who desires a fulfilled and expansive life. That "inner hunger" has led me to do a great deal of work on myself. I have spent a number of years in therapy, become a licensed spiritual consultant, graduated from two masters programs, one in spiritual psychology and one in consciousness studies and become a minister. I started noticing that the work that I had done personally absolutely mirrored the work that I was doing with my clients. In the last 12 years, I have counseled thousands of people, facilitated workshops and seminars and been a keynote speaker for National organizations. I decided to start documenting my process and the information that has come to and through me in support of helping others.

When I began working with people I started seeing that they would come in feeling stuck, inhibited, unable to express and unable to live the life they could see in their minds. There was gap between their dreams and how to have a fulfilling life. I started to explore avenues to support people in bridging that gap. Together we worked to uncover how old wounds, old hurts and old familial experiences kept them locked in patterns that they could not surpass.

It is my intention to support people in being free of old conditions, beliefs, and feelings of oppression that have kept them hostage in situations. This book is a "workbook for life change." You can use the information I present, and at the same time do the exercises to expand and facilitate healing.

This is what I know. When we are living from an intellectual understanding, it is not a point of healing. It is just an understanding of a concept. The actual healing takes place through the **experience** of health and well being, joy and clarity. Often times we attend workshops, read books and listen to lectures that leave us feeling high and inspired. Then, within a short time, we experience confusion because we do not understand how to use that information to stay focused and enjoy happy living. We are not clear on how to implement the tools in our lives beyond everyday challenges.

I want you to know that you have the tools to change. My intention is to create a place where you can feel supported and can anchor powerful tools as a transforming experience. This book is for students and people who are on a journey of growth and expansion. This book is for seekers of truth that are looking for tools to make more powerful choices and experience exciting advances in their life—in fact, changing their life completely.

I am so delighted you are reading this book because it shows you've made a choice to embrace life. So I honor your choice. Your willingness to change the way you experience life allows the Universe to stand in perfect alignment, to support and nurture you. **You** have created an opportunity to step beyond the circumstances blocking your freedom, making you feel stuck. This is a beginning, a time of renewal, and a chance to discover the truth of who you are. This is the dawning of an understanding: you are a **Co-Creator** with Spirit and today you choose to do things differently.

This book was created as a seven-week program to guide you on this new path. Please realize, you do not have to complete this program in seven weeks. If you get to a specific exercise where you want to explore more deeply or just be with your feelings, perfect. It is important for you to move toward your personal freedom in a way that supports your personal rhythm.

If you are working with a therapist or spiritual counselor, enlist their support as you process the program. They will be a wonderful resource for overcoming emotional blocks.

The human experience is filled with situations and circumstances that leave us feeling wounded. We have no power over misguided, disturbed, or mentally unbalanced individuals. We have little power, especially as children, in controlling or fighting off those who mentally, emotionally, or physically overpower us. It is often confusing and terrifying when parental figures, caretakers, lovers, or friends treat us in harmful or abusive ways. They are the very people who are supposed to be our protectors and comforters. Realizing this is not the truth, we are disheartened and disillusioned. Then we make decisions not to trust those nearest to us and these decisions can have far-reaching results. Such decisions anchor the belief that we are alone and not safe in this world. This can lead to anger and rage, controlling our relationships for years. These feelings are real and must be acknowledged.

I am not here to tell you to "get over it," "move on," "pretend nothing happened," or "remember that you are a Spiritual being and turn it over." All of these statements can act to bypass what we need: to acknowledge our fears, secrets, and painful experiences as stepping-stones to personal empowerment.

## "Healing is an evolutionary process not an end result."

Few of us leap to peaceful states of consciousness and enlightenment, especially, when we feel hurt or traumatized. We can, however, begin to understand that nothing from the past has to define the future.

It is often said, we are spiritual beings having a human experience. In the human realm, feeling wounded, abused, or abandoned is one of life's greatest challenges. Often we forget there is an unharmed space within us. Through the connection to an inner knowing, an all powerful Spirit and dynamic Universe we hear a call to us. The messages are, "Remember who you are." "Remember you are loved." "Remember, beyond all hurt, there is God."

# HOW TO
# USE THIS BOOK

Please be gentle with yourself during this program. There will be times when it may feel challenging or hard to continue. This is a natural part of healing and is to be expected. This **resistance** is simply a part of you afraid to step into the unknown. Bless and embrace this part and do the assignment anyway. This old way of being has served you up to this point. It is not your enemy. In fact, you will learn to understand the hidden beliefs and behavioral patterns belying your survival techniques. The commitment you make is the foundation for the healing. The more you honor this commitment and acknowledge your fears, the faster the process of healing will unfold. This book was created to be interactive. It is experiential in nature because it is very important that you practice what you are learning. That is how the tools will become an embodiment.

I have personally experienced and applied each process, as have many of my clients and workshop participants. Each section will begin with a blend of my personal experience and information I gleaned through various courses, workshops, and spiritual practice. I hope that sharing my personal unfolding will help you know you are not alone. I have also included personal stories written by people in their own words who have used spiritual principles to transform their lives. It is our hope that you will gain insight by the vulnerability of their sharing.

You will need a journal (a notebook is fine).

I encourage you to pick a **quiet space** and a **specific time** every day to focus on your healing. This is your time and you are worth it. Feel free to write down your thoughts, feelings, realizations, and revelations as often as possible. This will enhance your work with the weekly exercises.

The first exercise each week will open you to a deeper understanding of aspects calling for healing or expansion. You will be asked to sit still, breathe, and participate in a meditative exercise. The same meditations are on the enclosed CD if you choose not to do them on your own by reading the book. Each meditation on the CD is titled to correspond with the chapter and exercise. Immediately following each meditation is an instrumental version to support you in anchoring the meditation and suggested writing.

I have included questions to assist you in anchoring and help you complete the exercises. We are always asking questions that inspire the Universe to respond. Universal laws react to us from a neutral place. Usually we ask questions from an unconscious space and they often have a negative bent. If we ask negative questions like "Why does this always happen to me?" or "Why am I always getting hurt?" the answers will come back to us affirming the question. If you take away the "why" part of the question, what is left is the opportunity to build an affirmation. If we ask in a manner showing we are open to new possibilities and to connecting with parts of ourselves we have disowned, our way of being in the world shifts dramatically.

The **daily affirmations** will help you remember that your growth is the most important thing happening now. **You** are the priority. You are acting on a leap of faith and have indicated you are ready to make a change. Feel free to make notes on the affirmation pages.

The weekly **assignments** will open new ways of perceiving your life experiences and creating new patterns of living. Ultimately, you will be free to embody the peace of mind, joy, and depth of love for self and others you have long desired. Remember, you have all the tools within you. Take wing and soar into the vast arena of beauty that is **you**. I hold you in my heart and in my prayers.

Before you do one more thing,
remember...


You are a
masterpiece
of the Divine!

# WEEK ONE
# THE STORY

*"There is a pattern of perfection at the center of your being which has never been touched by disease or misfortune. Your intellect senses this through intuition, your imagination feels it by divine right, your inward consciousness knows it through faith. What you are trying to do is to awaken your whole being to spiritual awareness."*
~Ernest Holmes, **This Thing Called You** *(page 73)*

As I begin to write my life story it feels like I'm telling someone else's story, because I have moved so far from where I once was. I've undergone a transformation and healing, yet I'm clear about how those beginning life experiences molded me into who I am today. They allowed me to experience living in a deeper and richer way.

I was born in Minneapolis, Minnesota. My mother came from a family of four in Alabama. My father was born in Tennessee. He left my mother early in their relationship, right around the time I was born. So, my mother and my grandmother raised me. Mary, my grandmother, was quite interesting. She raised four children by herself in the South and managed to hold on to her land and feed and clothe her children. Ultimately, she migrated to Minnesota and her four children eventually joined her.

My mother, a beautiful, charming, lighthearted woman, was born in a time when the unspoken rule was that you had to be in a relationship to be happy or considered respectable. You had to be taken care of, especially if you weren't feeling whole within yourself. The thing to do was to get married. So that's what she did.

The first few years of my life, Mom struggled to make ends meet. She lived with my grandmother, feeling stuck and stagnant. After the marriage to my father failed, she was desperate to move away from the family and start a new life for the two of us. So she married my stepfather. I was five years old when we moved from Minneapolis to his home in St. Paul. My mother thought that getting away from her mother would provide independence and a life of her own. Unfortunately, she married a man who was not conscious and who was violent and abrasive. He was close to his sister and her children. There really wasn't much space for us to fit and create family.

I was a mouthy child, exuberant and independent by nature. My personality did not fit in that house. It was like oil and water trying to mix. I was constantly in trouble and received spankings. I remember on many occasions waking up to my mother and stepfather yelling and screaming. One night when mom was pregnant with my brother, I listened to him beating her. I entered their room and remember her saying in a terrified voice, "Get back to bed." Today I am clear she was protecting me. At the time, everything in me wanted to do something to stop the anger and protect my mother. Eventually, my mother woke up and left, but we both had deep and enduring emotional scars.

Most of the years after seven are foggy. My teen years are another story. They were challenging. I spent a lot of time trying to hide the insecurities. Trying to hide the fact that I did not think I was smart. Trying to hide the fact that there were secrets in my consciousness that I did not want anybody to know and so, I would be active in school affairs and worked very hard to be popular. We didn't have money so I knew I had to make myself visible. I became a model for a department store, joined the debate and chess teams and sang in school programs. I was always active but the truth is, I was trying to find myself by getting validation from these groups or from these experiences because I wanted people to think I was intelligent. I wanted people to think that I was powerful. I thought that if I could do all of these things people would notice me and tell me the truth of how wonderful I was. I experienced success through my singing, writing and my class work. However, it was never enough. The validation, the support and the acknowledgement could never fill that hole because underneath I was really convinced that I was not worthy. I was really convinced that I was not enough. I kept waiting for the other shoe to drop. I kept waiting for people to find out I was a fake. I kept waiting for people to find out that I was a phony. I kept waiting for people to find out that I really did not have anything to say because I really did not believe in myself.

Most of my adult life is also hazy, as I was emotionally asleep or tuned out. In my twenties and thirties, I went through a series of relationships that didn't support me. There were far too many unavailable and abusive men. I lived a life where discomfort was handled with drinking, smoking grass, or sleeping with people I didn't care about. Such activities were in the name of fun or partying. The truth is I was numbing myself.

After one really challenging relationship, I decided it was time to enter therapy. I had been on a spiritual path for some time, reading books, going to church and attending numerous workshops. I was searching for answers.

## Intuitively, I knew it was time to change the way I had been living.

I found a therapist and dived into the process, expecting to find out I needed to do some healing. What I didn't expect were the memories flooding in that made no sense to me. The realization and recognition of being physically abused as a child, caused a space of vulnerability unlike any I had ever known. By choosing therapy, I decided to look at my issues instead of running from them. My therapist was amazing and supportive of my spiritual path. He created a really safe space for me to express. I also enlisted the prayers and guidance of wonderful spiritual counselors and practitioners in Religious Science.

This part of the journey was extraordinarily difficult. The good news was my mother was still alive. As I remembered things, I could talk to her, although it was not comfortable for her or me. She affirmed the reality of my memories. They happened. She was mortified I had any memory of the horrible events. She presumed I was too young to remember. Some of the information was new for her, but she could not deny the possibility because my recollections were too vivid. I remember feeling so enraged. Why hadn't she taken care of me? Why had she allowed us to be in a situation where this man could physically, mentally, and emotionally abuse us?

Today, I realize I was absolutely gifted. Through prayer and deepening my spiritual practice, I had an opportunity to heal. That is the message of this book.

This is my story. This is the way it used to be. This story no longer runs my life. Abusive relationships, numbing out, running, feeling afraid, inability to stand up and be authentic or speak from a voice of power—these are no longer in my day-to-day reality. I transformed. Today, I come before you as the divine being I have always been. I have taken charge of my life and allow my destiny to unfold in a powerful way.

I love having this opportunity to share my journey and the tools supporting me. I am excited you are open to embracing your health, well-being, and unique destiny.

## MARY'S STORY – AGE 21

I have lived in Colorado my entire life. My childhood is somewhat vague. I don't remember very much at all. I know we had good times. For some reason I remember the bad times more. My first memory in life is sexual. My sister is 12 years older and she is touching me. She was getting raped by her step-dad at the time. I honestly don't think she knew any better.

My biological dad had always been prone to drinking. On occasion, he would act out. He would hit my brother more than me... and much harder than me. My brother always got in front of me. He tried to protect me. I don't know where my mom was on those nights. I simply don't remember. It felt like it went on forever... and then my aunt called Social Services.

My mom left when I was 13 years old. She was unhappy with my dad. They never had a great relationship. We didn't hear anything from her for a while and then we saw her occasionally. She was slowly cracking up, doing drugs and drinking on a regular basis.

Our house was really out of control. My dad was never around. He was drinking more than ever. We had huge parties all the time. There was a lot of booze and a lot of small drugs. I wasn't into it. I wasn't doing any of it until I got raped. It was at our house by my brother's best friend. I didn't tell anyone. Not right away. When I finally did my dad and brother didn't believe me. We had known that kid forever. They took his word over mine. He was always around. I didn't know what to do so I ran away, started doing drugs and started cutting myself with a knife. I told my mom about everything but she wasn't doing very well. She had been raped a lot growing up... and she just couldn't handle what I was telling her. After our conversation, she tried to drink herself to death and I found her. I moved in with my friend, her mom and her sister. They supported me a lot.

The bottom line is that things were crazy back then. Things continued to be really messed up for a long time....and in some ways they still are. I'm 21 years old now and feel as if I have grown up a lot. I more or less know what I want my life to consist of. I know how I want to live.

## I think the only way to make sense of it all is to transform the pain into something positive.

I want to help people. I want to spend every single day of my life building a better world. To say I've completely healed would be a lie.

I honesty think things happen the way they're supposed to. I think it's about using them for something bigger than you. It is about seeing God's plan in your life and not using problems as an excuse to self-destruct. It has been slow going—especially for me. But I'm whole heartedly committed to using my past for something much bigger.

# Week One
# Day One

# ARE YOU REALLY
# READY TO CHANGE?

How many times have you told your story? You know, the story of your painful childhood; the story of the lovers who have abandoned you; the story of the bad luck permeating every area of your life. Or that you are a failure and your dreams will never materialize.

Have you noticed that your family and friends are tired of your stories? They encourage you to seek a new way of looking at things? Is the story even boring to you, hearing yourself reciting it over and over again? Have you noticed that you feel fatigued and drained when you relate the story? OR do you find yourself reliving the experiences with the same intensity every time you tell it? Are you getting some pleasure from showing how others have caused you pain and are to blame for your circumstances? Does it feel good to be clear that you are the victim and others have mistreated you?

The real question is:

## Are you ready to let go of the story
## and move on?

If the answer is yes, this is your opportunity to tell it for the **last** time.

MEDITATION: (CD Track #2)

Get still for a few moments, close your eyes, and allow the breath to relax you. Inhale warm light and exhale tightness or anxiety anywhere in the body. Wherever you feel tight, let the light touch that part of the body and exhale. (Meditation music and candles may help). Continue to breathe in the light and exhale any tension until you feel calm. When you are relaxed, begin to write your story.

Here are the steps:

1.  Use as many sheets of paper as you need. (Do not write this in your journal). Do not leave out any details. Do not hold back. This is for your eyes only, so there is nothing you cannot say. Take as long as you like to make sure you get it all out. You might consider answers to the following questions:

❖ What was my childhood experience?

❖ How did I respond to events that felt unsupported?

❖ How has my life reflected the continuation of childhood events?

❖ What choices have I made that mirrored the circumstances of my life?

❖ What did I come to believe about others and myself?

2. When you feel complete, say the following.

> *"I surrender. Today, I choose to let go of anything that holds me hostage to the past. Today, I step into the present and embrace it fully!"*

3. Use this week as an opportunity to add things to the story. Your daily quiet time is perfect for reflection and expressing more details. It is important to get all of this on paper. Keep the story on your altar or in a safe place. We will do a completion exercise at the end of this program.

# Day Two

# OBSERVER #1

Today, I stand back as the observer. I watch the number of times my story wants to come forward and be told. I observe the number of times I may want to communicate the dramas of my life. I watch as I tell others of my misfortunes.

There is nothing to do. I simply watch.

**AFFIRMATION:**

*"I am awakening to new ways of being. I bless every part of me. I know that my ability to see every aspect of who I am is the beginning of my freedom!"*

# Day Three

# OBSERVER #2

As I step into this day, I stand in gratitude. I experience my feelings and I am clear that something within me is moving. This is an opportunity to view, from the space of an observer, my thoughts, actions, and patterns.

How good it is to realize that there is nothing to judge. There is no right or wrong here. I simply behold the process and acknowledge my willingness to grow.

**AFFIRMATION:**

*"There is a power in me that is greater than my fears. I tap into this power today and allow my inner strength to fully emerge!"*

## Day Four

# HALFWAY DAY

I acknowledge myself and my desire to change. I applaud my willingness to move through the rest of this week with ease. I ask for support from God and the Universe in realizing my full potential.

I experience the power of keeping this commitment with myself.

**AFFIRMATION:**

*"I celebrate myself today and move through this day gracefully!"*

## Day Five

# CHANCE TO CHOOSE

I choose this day to hold back my need to share my story. I choose to empower the truth of my life. I am an amazing Spiritual being and I am opening to the life I so richly deserve.

Today, I allow my silence to be a statement of my commitment to change. I take time to explore how situations in my life may be opportunities for growth.

**AFFIRMATION:**

*"I stand in the strength of my resolve. I claim victory over my past and I taste the joy of releasing the past!"*

## Day Six

# LETTING GO

I dedicate this day to letting go. As thoughts and feelings arise, I acknowledge their presence and gently ask them to leave in support of my growth. I clearly state that I am the master of my destiny and I surrender the need to dwell in the past.

I ask Spirit to take any thoughts or feelings weighing me down and ask for assistance in releasing old beliefs.

**AFFIRMATION:**

*"I let go and let God take my fears, doubts and anxieties. I rest in the awareness that I am free in God's love! I am at peace!"*

## Day Seven

# TAKING ACTION #1

Take a moment to recognize the powerful inner work you have accomplished this week. It has taken commitment and conscious attention. Bravo. You are awesome!

**MEDITATION:**

**Once again, quiet yourself and allow your breath to relax you. Think about the revelations that came forward this week.**

**Once you feel relaxed, list each challenge you have experienced in your life and next to it write a possible opportunity for learning about yourself. This is a chance to gain clarity in how a belief has factored into your life.**

**Write whatever comes to mind. Don't edit. It is important to put on paper what has come forward this week.**

Examples:

CHALLENGES

**OPPORTUNITY FOR LEARNING**

I attract unavailable men.

**My father was like the men I choose.**

Angry people upset me.

**I don't know how to deal with my own rage.**

My father abused me.

**I am afraid to trust.**

My mother is controlling.

**I feel the need to be in control to feel safe.**

I feel helpless.

**I am afraid to speak my truth.**

**When this is complete say the following:**

**AFFIRMATION:**

*"I take full responsibility for my life and my behavior. I take the attention off others and place it fully on myself. I am changing now!"*

# WEEK TWO
# FINDING YOUR VOICE

*The caged bird sings with a fearful trill of things unknown but longed for still and his tune is heard on the distant hill for the caged bird sings of freedom.*

~*Maya Angelou,* **The Caged Bird Sings**

Such an interesting concept: finding your voice. It took me a long time to realize I even had a voice. I spent most of my life in relationships and in various jobs where I did not believe I had any power or that my opinion would be heard. When hired for jobs, I thought, "I've fooled them and sooner or later someone is going to find out I'm incapable and not worthy. They'll find out I don't know what I'm doing and have nothing important to say." I spent a lot of time covering my tracks and trying to fit in. I witnessed other people doing creative and successful things and I emulated them so they would think I was smart and belonged.

Operating from such an uncomfortable place turned my fear into reality. People treated me in ways that mirrored my thoughts about myself—I was not worthy of being powerful. I often felt abused. The more I tried to fit in the more challenging situations would become. When I finally got the courage to honestly share my thoughts or my feelings, I'd have a pain in my throat and my jaw got tight. Immediately following the pain came tears. I started to believe that in order to get the feelings out beyond the pain a form of attack or rage was required. I constantly felt victimized and wanted everyone to know I needed to be heard. It didn't work because all people saw was the rage and it was scary for them. Finally, one day I realized that if I was going to be heard, (which is the calling of every individual), I had to find another way to communicate. I had to share from the heart and not from the fear I carried around as old baggage.

I began to explore ways to reveal my authentic self. I was determined to find a way to express my feelings, get what I needed, and not be afraid someone would leave if I spoke honestly. It wasn't a beautiful or easy process. Some moments I was extraordinarily successful and other moments I failed miserably. But my commitment to find my voice was the portal to freedom. Slowly, I began to trust myself and learn skills for communicating without blame and anger. Today, I am still learning, but I'm not afraid to show people who I am. I'm not afraid to say what I want, what I need, or what I think. I learned to listen to myself and to others. I developed an understanding that every person has value and has something to contribute.

If God is for us, who or what can be against us? If we live in a Universe of good, how can there be anything to fear? These two questions offer an opportunity to explore the true nature of our being. If there is nothing to fear, we must come to understand that worry, concern, and anxiety come from our individual perceptions of separation or lack. We need to shift our perceptions from limitation to infinite possibility.

So why do we hang on to fear? What is the payoff for clutching to things that made me feel bad or behave in unsupportive ways? Every moment is a moment of choice. Every moment is an opportunity to practice the presence of Spirit as the life we live. Why not begin today to let go and let God shine fully as you? Why not stop talking about speaking authentically and just do it. Do it for you! It is my joy to assist you in finding **your** true and powerful voice.

## SHIRLEY'S STORY – AGE 57

**A**/meaning one /**L**/lost one /**O**/own self /**N**/ to negate own self/ **E**/eternity forever be. I lost myself for a fleeting second/ only to find myself in me/ a woman/ girl/ a child/ a baby/ one/one/ me.

The above poem was written by a woman/child in her early twenties, a "cry for help" a fragmented soul trying to merge, heal her spirit and find her voice/song. This journey has taken thirty years to find full expression.

My stepfather was a brilliant man; Mom would always send me to him if I needed math homework. I would plead with her to help me and she would say, go ask James he's much better at math than me. James would talk you through a problem and when you didn't quite get it and had a question he would say, "You're stupid or any moron could get this. If you listened you would get it."

I had a mother who always encouraged me to do my best and be goal oriented. I got A and B's in school. Very seldom were any of my accomplishments celebrated. I was very active in school winning numerous awards, voted to the student body and was popular in school. Whatever I set my intentions on I achieved.

In the house of fear, I could not express my feelings or have an opinion about the world. If I shared a moment with my mother and told her about an adventure or about my day in school, the imitator (stepfather) walked through the room and said things like, "That's bullshit!" or "Stop lying!"

Sometimes my mom answered, "She just has a vivid imagination."

"Yeah, it sounds to me like she doesn't know what the hell she is talking about," he replied.

While I fought in the home to be seen and heard, I also fought outside the home. The time was the early sixties and our family moved off the Air Force base and integrated an all white neighborhood. I had to adapt and fight through all of the racial epitaphs of that period. I adapted by developing a mask of humor. I made people laugh to hide the pain, doubt and self-esteem insecurities that lay beneath my smile.

I was adjusting and had made friends with my white school mates in elementary school. But my last year of Jr. High School was a living hell. The district began to bus the black children to my school. Up until that time, I was the only person of color. The black kids couldn't understand the relationship I already had with my white friends. How could they know? All they saw was a black girl befriended by white people. The name calling had started all over again, "Oreo cookie, ya' think ya' betta than us, Nigga ya' white nigga." The black kids used to follow me home taunting and name calling the way the white kids had done years before. I remember coming home from school one day crying to my mother and asking her for help. "Am I supposed to be their friends because I am the same color, I don't know those girls calling me names, *WHAT AM I GOING TO DO?*"

My mother told me, "That it was something you will have to work out on my own."

That's what I did; I befriended the leader, Helen Davis. She taught me how to survive in the streets. I learned how to "be black" from her. I learned to assimilate and imitate other voices for I was unsure of my own. I paid homage to all the tribes, spoke their language, became them while I was with them. I was with them and belonged to none of them. When I would walk into the cafeteria, I had to go to the Black table first, talk jive and laugh. Then I would excuse myself saying I was going to get a sticky bun, on my way I stopped at the white table to commune with the kids I first befriended in elementary school; then I would get my sticky bun and stop by the table with the "others," the Spanish and Asian students.

The final confrontation and years of abuse came to a head one afternoon. I was on restriction again and I had disobeyed the order to come straight home. I chose instead to meet my boyfriend after school. As fate would have it my boyfriend and I were crossing the street and the first car to stop and let us by the cross walk was my stepfather. I was petrified. He said nothing and drove the car off. I took the bus home in dread. As soon as I reached the door I was greeted by my stepfather and the brown belt he always beat me with. He began to beat me...I snapped.

I thought I am seventeen. When does the abuse stop?

I began to hit him back. I screamed, "I'm glad that you're not my father and I'm sick of you hurting me!"

He said, "I'm glad too."

The minute I heard this, the floodgates of rejection, rage and pain came pouring out of every cell in my body. The wound had been ripped and reopened. I fought like a wild animal wanting to hurt him like he had hurt me.

He stopped beating me with the belt and began using his fists. We both fought, hand to hand combat going from the living room into the kitchen, then into the den where my mother was sitting. I look at her defeated. I was crying and begging with my eyes for her to intervene and make it stop. She turned her head away from my helpless gaze. I was alone.

The next day my mother walked into the room and told me that he would not put his hands on me again. It was too late. I couldn't trust any longer. I began to seek what I thought was love though physical contact, mistaking sex for love. For the next twenty-five years, I struggled to break free.

When I re-read my "wound" story, I knew it was a story that I had held on to for many years. I can now look back from a place of understanding. I have let go of the story.

It did not come over night, but has come as a result of the living, laughing, dying and crying experiences of life. I am no longer standing in judgment and viewing it from my inner child's point of view. It was when I could detach and see my mother, father and step-father as people who also had a story that I began understanding them through my own personal life experiences.

When I had enough of allowing relationships to dictate who I was just to be accepted and stifle my voice, when I tired of lying down and rolling over being submissive just to be accepted as someone's friend, when I stopped running away from the voice within that abused me and judged me, I decided to let go.

I let go of the fear, stopped running from it and decided to begin to understand it by viewing the circumstance, events, the people and the historical period from a place of detachment. No, it did not diminish the abuse that was done to me. It provided a portal for me to find ways to nurture and love my inner child and heal her childhood wound.

When I began taking care of her and loving her, something changed, I began to walk in the world differently. I started to be present with myself and with others. My inner life became more important to me. I became strong for her. I had a purpose. **Me.**

I had to heal because I finally realized that I was important.

## No one could love me enough to heal me.

I had to love me for that to happen. Slowly, by going within, I began hearing a distant voice; I will call it my God voice guiding me. I started listening to that voice which guided me. Serendipitous meetings and events started presenting themselves and they gave me answers to my healing journey.

I am still learning to trust and listen to that voice.

## Week Two
## Day One

# FINDING YOUR OWN VOICE

How do you deal with your emotions? Do you have emotional outbursts that seem to come from nowhere? Do you choose to keep quiet even though you are filled with anger and resentment? Are you afraid to upset people? Do you put up a wall so no one can get close enough to hurt you? Do you feel no one really understands you? If you answered "yes" to any of these questions, it might be time to learn some tools for expressing your thoughts, needs, desires and concerns in a constructive way. Suppressing anger, frustration, or disappointments denies you the opportunity to fully express. Raging out of control depletes your energy and pushes people away.

Unresolved rage is one of the major causes of mental, emotional and physical challenges. It can outpicture as emotional eating, violence to self or others, isolating behavior, drug or alcohol addiction and inappropriate sexual behavior. It is connected to the inability to express feelings in healthy ways. This is learned behavior because many of us were punished or abused when we spoke up or questioned behavior that seemed unsupportive. So, the reaction has been to implode and stuff emotions.

We will dedicate this week to finding your voice. The intention is to discover how to communicate your feelings in an empowering way using creative means. There are no rules. You can write poems, draw or paint your feelings, compose a song, make a collage of your feelings, write or draw with your non-dominant hand, or cut pictures out of magazines and make a book of feelings.

## MEDITATION: (CD Track #3)

Sit in a comfortable position. Make sure you have your journal with you. You might want to put on some inspiring and comforting music. Close your eyes and begin to breathe slowly and easily. Each breath will create a space for you to receive information. Each breath will support you in listening to your inner-most self. Open your mind to memories, events, or circumstances where you felt powerless or immobilized. Connect to the moments when you could not find your voice. Whatever is there, let it come forward. If there is sadness, allow it to be there. If feelings of shame or guilt emerge, let it be all right. If you feel angry, allow it to come up. Trust that in this moment you are safe. If you feel stuck, ask yourself the following questions:

❖ What emotion is attached to this memory?

❖ What have I always wanted to say or do relative to this person or event?

❖ What stopped me from expressing fully in that moment?

When everything has been expressed, open your eyes and write down what is present. When you are complete say the following:

*"Today I embrace myself fully. I express my feelings in constructive, supportive ways. I look within and recognize I am loved and supported just the way I am!"*

Each day this week, you will spend your quiet time creatively expressing the feelings you just wrote about. Commit to a small creative project. (Note: For any over-achievers, relax and just play).

Allow yourself the freedom of expression so vivid in children. Allow your imagination to run wild. Draw a picture, write a poem or play with clay. Explore your creative nature. It is unlimited. This is all about learning to get your feelings out in a new way.

I have included two of my drawings and one of my paintings. For the drawings, I used my non-dominant hand to open the creative side of the brain. The painting is from a dream class that I took to re-create dreams and their meanings.

*Dream Painting*

*My desire for my mother, brother & myself*

*1996*

*Hostage - no more!*

*1996*

## Day Two

# BIRTHING THE ARTIST

Today, I allow the artist within me to step forward. I rejoice in the opportunity to create in a way that has always wanted to express. I set the intention to open the floodgates of my creativity.

Today, I begin to tap the depths of my emotions through art. I give myself permission to give birth to every aspect of my feelings.

**AFFIRMATION:**

*"Divine guidance leads me to inspiring spaces within myself. I am grateful for the opportunity to begin anew!"*

## Day Three

# THE GIFTS

I witness with awe the desires to be expressed. I do not hold back in any form. I am committed to revealing the emerging thoughts and visions.

I listen to my inner voice and allow my gifts to explode in my consciousness.

**AFFIRMATION:**

*"I lovingly release old wounds. I choose freedom now as my creativity fully reveals itself. I hold nothing back!"*

## Day Four

# BREAKING THE MOLD

I call forth any and all beliefs that have held me hostage. I explore news ways to release the pain of my past.

Today, I discover new ideas as I expand my level of awareness. As I creatively express them, I am clear that I am being transformed.

**AFFIRMATION:**

*"I am a creative being and the paths of expression are infinite. I allow Spirit to express through me now... beyond boundaries!"*

## Day Five

# OUTSIDE THE LINES

This day, I step into the awareness that there are no limits to my creativity. New forms of articulating my thoughts reveal themselves effortlessly.

I dare to tell the truth that sets me free.

**AFFIRMATION:**

*"Today I realize there are no limitations in God. Nothing blocks my brilliance or my ability to fulfill my intention!"*

# Day Six

# COMPLETION

As I complete my project I give thanks for my fortitude. I am grateful for my strength and willingness to speak my truth.

I honor myself and the creative Spirit within.

**AFFIRMATION:**

*"I joyously bask in my love of God as I celebrate my Co-Creation with Spirit."*

## Day Seven

# TAKING ACTION #2

Stop in this moment and honor the creative genius you are. You have taken a major step in releasing unsupportive patterns and beliefs. Congratulations!

This is a time of reflection. Take a moment to look at your project, to see what you have completed. Acknowledge yourself and what has moved into form. Begin to breathe slowly, experience the feeling of becoming still. If your mind is racing, breathe until you feel relaxed. Give thanks for the revelations that came forward this week. Now review the week in your mind and contemplate what you have learned. When you feel centered, write down what is present for you in your journal. Be sure to document any differences in your feelings. This is important. Take as long as you feel is necessary to put the feelings on paper. When you are finished, say the following affirmation:

*"My emotions are not in control of my life. In this moment, I choose to embrace positive and empowering ways to communicate my feelings to myself and others!"*

Creativity is a wonderful tool to release energy. I encourage you to continue to explore creative ways to free your life of old behaviors and beliefs that don't support you. Music, painting, writing, and movement are all avenues to freedom. It is important to allow your personal creativity to emerge without judgment. You are unique and so is the way you express. The creative energy of Spirit is unlimited. Why not co-create with the Divine in wonderful and freeing ways?

# WEEK THREE
# CONNECTING
# MIND & BODY

*Your physical body is surrounded by an energy field that extends as far out as your outstretched arms and the full length of your body. It is both an information center and a highly sensitive perceptual system.*
*~Carolyn Myss,* **Anatomy of the Spirit** *(page 33)*

Mind-body connection was one of the most challenging areas for me. When I got scared as a child, I left my body mentally and emotionally. I couldn't connect to simple movements. I couldn't command my body to do what I saw in my mind. It was as if I had two completely different parts acting out my life. This was really challenging since I am African American and we "are all supposed to know how to dance." Imagine my dismay when I would be at a party and would lose the beat and be out of sync with everyone else. I was mortified and would often find myself sitting on the sidelines so that people wouldn't see how uncoordinated I truly was.

When I felt threatened in any way, I became immobilized. I was like an animal being attacked, but instead of running, I surrendered. It was as if I had no will of my own. It was many years later that I discovered a psychological term for this behavior, *disassociation*. When the environment feels too threatening, people who have been abused or traumatized often experience this form of disconnect.

As a performer and actress, I was challenged by disassociation. There were moments when I was connected and brilliant. Other times I couldn't find a way to be fully present during an audition or a performance. Feedback from instructors, directors, and producers varied. It all depended upon which "me" they experienced; the one fully in my body or the one who had vacated the space because of a fear.

One day, I auditioned for a part and was confident. The character was perfect for me and all I had to do was show up. My agent told me that there was a special request for me and that I had a great chance. I walked into the room. The reception from the casting director, director and producers was warm and inviting. I centered myself and began to read. All of a sudden, I felt light headed and disconnected. I asked if I could begin again. They were very accommodating. I began to read and realized in that instant that something was happening beyond my control. I finished the reading. It was horrible. I left the room feeling dismayed. As I walked down the hall, I began to realize that I was crying but I couldn't feel it. It was as if I was experiencing myself cry but I couldn't feel a thing.

Although aware of the challenge of disconnecting, I felt helpless to do anything about it. I dated an actor involved in the practice of yoga and he invited me to attend a class. It was an amazing experience. I was in touch with my body for the first time. Needless to say, I was hooked. I went twice a week and was overjoyed with the feeling of being in touch with my body. One day, at the end of class, I felt lightheaded. I walked outside and had difficulty standing. I felt afraid and saw pictures in my mind that made no sense.

My therapist explained that through yoga I had become physically strong enough to face some buried fear. The movement had re-activated my old survival mechanism locked in the memory of the cells in my body. They had kicked into gear to protect me from re-experiencing the trauma. However, I realized that I was at choice. I could move forward and uncover the area requiring attention or I could stop working on my body. There was no way I was going to stop. I continued yoga. The fear intensified.

I had to convince myself to open my body enough to heal the old wounds. I was directed to a trainer, Eddie Wilde, specializing in working with people who had been traumatized. I was put on a strict diet and worked out five to six days a week.

Several months later, I was in the gym lying on my back and Eddie was spotting me as I lifted a weight bar above my chest. Suddenly, the room changed and I had the experience of someone being on top of me. I froze. Eddie talked to me, saying this memory wanted to come out. I wanted to run, but he encouraged me not to give up. We were close to a breakthrough. I cried all the way home and got in the shower to calm myself. I continued to cry, when all of a sudden I became aware of the water on my body. I was astonished! I was actually feeling the water on my body in a different way. It was as if I had never experienced a shower before.

The room became still and I had a revelation. Something happened to open my ability to actually feel my body. I began to wonder what other areas had been shut down. I was elated. What if I continued to strengthen my body, my mind, and my spirit at the same time? Would I be able to experience feeling my body completely? Would I be able to stay connected when I felt afraid? I jumped out of the shower with a new found excitement.

I have never been the same. My search for new ways to experience the mind-body connection has been extraordinarily powerful for me and important in supporting the hundreds of people I've worked with over the years.

I invite you to explore your own mind-body connection. This is an opportunity for you to unlock old patterns and beliefs that no longer serve you. This is the time to find the strength within yourself to stay present in every situation.

## TINA'S STORY – AGE 51

Our bodies are alive. You might in this moment be thinking, duh! But I invite you into considering your body in a way that takes you beyond your common understanding and experience of its aliveness. I encourage you to think of it as a partner, a lover, your child and friend.

This may sound odd but in the mid 1980's I experienced a series of events that brought about profound realizations that continue to deepen my relationship with my body and my life. At the time I had been suffering with a sprained ankle that just would not heal. I saw at least three doctors and a number of alternative health practitioners. I took steroids and natural remedies trying to heal and leave this injury behind. Nothing worked. Then, there came an odd, odd week of me accidentally hurting myself left and right—from stubbing my toe, to hitting my funny bone to bumping my knee and being racked with pain. Somewhere in this week (*from what I thought was hell*), heaven broke through. During one of those painful physical mishaps—when the pain shot out in all directions— without thinking I grabbed my injured limb and stroked it. I verbally expressed loving care to it. I said, "Oh. I am so sorry. I did not mean to hurt you." Yes, I said it out loud as though I was talking to a person that I loved rather than to "just" my body. Seconds later the pain was completely gone. It seemed to vanish almost magically. I could not feel any evidence to prove that pain existed just seconds earlier.

I fancy myself a spiritual scientist and this experience intrigued me. I wanted to know if it was just my imagination or was there really healing power in verbally speaking to myself in the midst of hurt or injury. I conducted my own very non-scientific tests.

Most of the time, when I hurt myself, I would be quick to touch the spot, acknowledge the pain and then offer it loving care and consideration by saying, "I am sorry," out loud. The words felt good to my heart and the pain usually vanished or at least the stinging pain was very short lived.

When I failed to respond and take care of me in this way the pain or injury lasted longer. At first I was surprised that this was the case and then it occurred to me that hearing another person acknowledge me through an apology always felt good to my soul. The apology had a way of making room for letting the whole thing—whatever it was—go! Could it be that the same behavior of apology and loving consideration of my body could make a profound difference in how and for how long my body held pain? Was it possible that my body had a responsive intelligence—that heard and responded to my voice and understood my words?

I began talking to my body frequently as though it was indeed my best friend. I gave special attention to my ankle. I told it I was sorry that I hurt it. I told it I was willing to do whatever was necessary to give it what it needed. I held it and even kissed it. It got better; then it healed completely. What at one time, for a period of over two years, was a tender spot filled with chronic pain is today healthy, strong and pain free.

Make of this story what you will.

## I have come to know that there is a mental me, a physical me, an emotional me and a spiritual me.

Each is intelligent and responsive.
Each is influenced by the other.
When all are aligned, I feel a powerful sense of wholeness. When they are not aligned, each does its best to guide me in the direction that brings us all together again.

Each responds to acts of love.

Today, when I hurt for any reason I have learned to first actively extend love to myself and tell the friend in me, that I am sorry that she hurts. I accept that my body is highly intelligent and knows what it needs and has its own way of communicating. I listen from the inside out to hear what it has to say. I regularly and verbally thank it for its strength, intelligence, responsiveness and balance. I speak openly to my body praising it and talking about being healthy until I die. When I do get sick, I listen deeply and follow the subtle guidance—telling me to rest, forgive and trust more. I am thrilled by my body's ability to fall asleep quickly and effortlessly night after night, and to sleep soundly and require only 5-6 hours of rest a night.

I am developing an active love affair with every part of me and it is paying off. My heart really is filled with joy, possibility and expectancy. I pray that I am in harmony with myself until the day I die.

Week Three
Day One

# FREE YOUR BODY

Your body is like a computer. Everything you've experienced is imprinted in your cells, muscles, and tissues. Many authors discuss the effect of the mind on the body and how thoughts and traumas can have long-lasting effects on the immune system.

Stop a moment and take inventory of your life. Have you noticed that you get sick at the same time every year? Does your body break down (cold, flu, back problems) in high stress situations? Do you have immobilizing headaches? Does your body feel fatigued and worn out when you have to do something challenging? Any or all of these can be traced to some emotional, mental, or physical act that impacted or traumatized you.

We will dedicate this week to finding ways to free your body gently. We will explore ways to discover and uncover old memories or wounds lodged in the body. You may already have a physical regimen and I encourage you to continue it.

## MEDITATION: (CD Track #4)

Sit and breathe.

Allow the breath to assist you in feeling the beauty of stillness. As you inhale, pay special attention to the places in your body feeling tense or tight. Do nothing but observe.

As you exhale, breathe out the tension in the body. Begin to feel you can have a dialogue with your body. Ask your body to reveal areas ready to be healed. Continue to breathe. Ask your body to connect you to the types of illnesses or body challenges appearing time and time again.

Look deeply.

It could be a chronic back problem or knee problems. Don't discount any challenge you experience in your body. Ask to see any patterns occurring in the body temple. Don't judge what you see or feel. This is just an exploration. Notice the places in your body that are tight. When you feel complete with this process, take out your journal and begin to write. Make sure you document the tight areas. These are message centers. Write about how your body reacts when emotions or life circumstances appear to be out of control. Do not edit here. Write without worrying about the form.

Consider the following questions:

❖　　What part of my body feels tight as I
　　　explore this area of my life?

❖　　What does the energy in this particular part
　　　of the body want to express?

❖　　What energy, illness, or challenge reoccurs
　　　in this part of my body?

❖　　Is there something important my body
　　　wants to express to support my healing?

When you feel complete with the writing say the following affirmation:

*"In this moment I choose to free my body from limiting thoughts and beliefs. I am freeing my body to be the fullest expression of health and well being God intended."*

Now choose one thing you will do physically every day for the next few days. It could be five minutes of stretching.

❖ It could be a walk. It could be yoga, spinning, aerobics, or just dancing to music in your living room.

❖ It's important that you commit to moving your body everyday for a minimum of 5 minutes (20 minutes would be ideal).

❖ Set an intention before each of these sessions to see and learn about blockages in your body with grace and ease. We don't want this to be hard.

After the movement each day, sit and listen to your body to create a dialogue. It will begin to inform you about how the tension relates to beliefs hindering your growth.

❖ At the end of each round of dialogue, write down your thoughts, feelings, or revelations.

❖ Feel free to write about your resistance. Whatever comes forward does not have to make sense or connect to anything. We will explore this at a later time.

## Day Two

# HONORING

Today, I commit to loving my body. I observe any resistance to honoring that commitment. I choose to step up and discover ways to expand my understanding of my body and its needs.

I honor myself, declaring my readiness to move forward. I am open as my body reveals its desires and secrets.

**AFFIRMATION:**

*"There is nothing standing in the way of my body fully supporting me. This is a glorious day as I step into the freedom of expressing my body's full potential."*

# Day Three

# ASKING

This day I am asking my body to open up blocked areas. As feelings come forward, I am clear they are answering this request.

I write about the experiences and give thanks for opening to the truth that will set me free.

**AFFIRMATION:**

*"I am centered in God. As I spiritually clean house, I delight in the emerging revelations. In any moment, I can stop and remember to breathe. I am one with my body now."*

## Day Four

# FEEDING THE BODY TEMPLE

I observe my eating habits today. I need do nothing but watch the number of times I crave unhealthy foods.

I watch my body as it reacts after each meal. I ask myself, "How do I feel?"

**AFFIRMATION:**

*"I am experiencing a shift in my consciousness. I look candidly at the foods I choose to eat. I claim my health now!"*

## Day Five

# CHECKING IN

This day is dedicated to observing what I feel while looking into the memory of my body. I am gentle with myself as I explore areas that may feel uncomfortable.

I lovingly acknowledge my willingness to face whatever is present.

**AFFIRMATION:**

*"I am courageous. I am powerful. My commitment to grow makes me strong."*

## Day Six

# NEW IDEAS

I dedicate this day to welcoming new ideas empowering my body. I pick up a book for new information. I take time to seek out individuals who can guide me to new understanding of my health and well being.

I am ready to embrace new ways to uplift myself.

**AFFIRMATION:**

*"I open to the infinite possibility of total health. I ask for and receive all I need to move beyond limitations in my body. I actively love my body now!"*

## Day Seven

# TAKING ACTION

Wow! You made it through a whole week of placing attention on your body. How wonderful. You deserve to be acknowledged.

Take some time to get still and breathe. Make this a time to honor yourself for the past week. When you feel totally relaxed, read through your writings for the past few days. Look at the patterns, feelings, and discoveries. Allow yourself to breathe in the information. Make sure you feel centered. You may have to close your eyes again and consciously relax each area of the body. When you are clear, write down "SELF-NURTURING," "PHYSICAL" and "FOOD." You are going to make a commitment in each area that you will continue for the next four weeks.

Do not commit to something you won't do. It is important to keep your word to yourself. As we develop trust within ourselves, we learn to trust others.

SELF-NURTURING—It could be a bath, reading, walking, seeing a movie, or watching a sunset. It should be something not related to work or your healing.

PHYSICAL—Some form of exercise. A minimum of three days a week would be ideal, but start where you feel comfortable. If it is once a week, that's great!

FOOD—Pick one challenging area and choose one thing you will commit to changing. It could be eating more fruit, cutting down on chocolate, or eating fewer carbohydrates.

When you are finished, say the following affirmation.

*"My commitment to myself is real. I deserve to be free and experience the total beauty of my body. I tap into my personal power now!"*

# WEEK FOUR
# SECRETS

*"Total surrender involves loving trust. You cannot surrender totally unless you trust lovingly and totally....The loving trust implies that we know the love of God and that we proclaim this love, compassion, and mercy everywhere we are sent."*
~*Mother Teresa,* **Total Surrender** *(pp.40-41)*

For many of us, trust is a **huge** block to freedom. We have been raised in families or entered into relationships where secrets denied us entry into intimacy and therefore, trust.

Throughout my childhood, I was aware of mistrust in my family. I couldn't quite put my mind around what was happening, but instinctively I knew of the invisible walls.

John Bradshaw wrote an illuminating book entitled *Family Secrets.* He wrote about the toxicity created through withholding secrets and discussed how patterns of denial, secrets, and betrayal can be passed down from generation to generation without being addressed.

While in a class at the University of Santa Monica, I was asked to track my genealogy in search of generational patterns. Fascinated with the assignment, I had numerous conversations with my mother and relatives about the family history and secured my grandmother's diaries. What I discovered was astonishing. Five generations of women in my family were physically and sexually abused. Many had been in multiple violent marriages and relationships. More importantly, **no one talked about it**. Everyone held pieces of the puzzle, but there was an agreement (spoken and unspoken) to withhold this information. No one realized that keeping secrets could be destructive, anchoring the patterns into the DNA to be passed on generation after generation.

In my case, I discovered that my mother had been locked in a small box in the heat for punishment as a child. When I was three years old, my babysitter locked me in a basement for punishment. Coincidence? Maybe, but many identical experiences occurred in both of our childhoods including violent beatings by our fathers (stepfather in my case).

I had an opportunity to stop the pattern, to stop the secrets holding me hostage. I enlisted the help of a friend and theatrical director to assist me in writing my story as a one-woman show. My intention was to be as authentic and honest as possible. It took several months of painful discovery to finish the play. As we began the rehearsal process, I had to move into a space of deep vulnerability to be successful. This practice of truth telling was scary, enlivening, intense, and cathartic. The first time we invited an audience to experience the release of my secrets, I was terrified. I had to choose to expose myself in a way I had never done before. At the conclusion of the performance, I felt totally free. Audience members were loving and acknowledging. They said it gave them permission to expose secrets keeping them imprisoned.

The play, entitled *The Hand of God,* traveled to many U.S. cities, opening a portal for audience members and for me to heal. After each performance, we held question and answer sessions. People were hungry to learn how to stop hiding. The "What Will Set You Free?" workshops began in Minneapolis at the Illusion Theater and currently support people in the discovery of freedom through authentic truth telling.

So now it's your turn. What an awesome time to begin and let go of anything separating you from the total trust of God, love and ultimately, yourself.

## LYNNETTE'S STORY - AGE 57

I always thought my mom was rational. But as a child, I grew up gravitating toward my dad, who manipulated and cultivated our relationship. Because he was physically abusive to my mom, it felt safer to align with him. So I was truly a "Daddy's girl" yet I knew my mom loved me dearly. In fact, she always felt too protective, too suspicious and too wary of others. When upset, she'd ramp up and spiral into an emotional rage that was terrifying to watch.

At first, I just accepted the way she was, but as I grew older I began to pull away. I really didn't feel connected to her, and didn't understand her. I knew she didn't understand me, but we formed a truce of pretending to get along.

Meanwhile, I learned that it was important to choose my words carefully – always leaving out any detail that might provoke her over-reaction. So I kept secrets – always – never letting her see my joys or hurts, for fear they'd be used against me. I became an adroit liar too.

Part of my world was watching my parents fight. It wasn't often, but enough to scare me whenever their voices started to rise. It usually meant my dad would grab my mom and back her against a wall or throw her on the bed – while they both struggled against each other.

They both say he never hit her, but that's not what I remember.

By the time I was 9 years old, my mom's spirit was fluctuating: sometimes she was a valiant warrior shutting down a restaurant for refusing to serve us, and sometimes she was a meek person who seemed hopeless and resigned. But that summer she decided to visit her parents in Chicago, and took me with her.

As we boarded the plane, she said she was leaving my dad for good – as if this was good news! I was horrified at the thought of only living with her and felt hopeless – kidnapped by my own mother.

We moved into my Grandparent's home. I listened to her rages against my dad, was bullied in school for being "different," and was present when her adult brother tried to molest a 10 year-old foster girl living with us.

The family way of dealing with trauma was to **"deny everything – pretend!"** I really began to think something was wrong with me. I'd refer to these events and was told they never happened. I "dreamed it" or "made it up."

## I believed that they wouldn't lie to me so it must be me, right?

I spent the next summer with my dad – relieved to be away from what I couldn't even describe. My dad encouraged me to mock and ridicule her behind her back with him, so my feelings were validated.

The second summer there, I refused to go back, and stayed with Dad to start Jr. High School. Mom never accepted that he had moved on – from her. She would show up unannounced—ostensibly to bring me things I'd need—but it was so clear she wanted to check on us. Each time they were sexual and she left hopeful. I knew better and I just wanted them to stay apart!

Once I finished Jr. High, I decided to go back to Chicago. As I started high school, my Mom's paranoia became evident, but as a kid I had no language for how serious it was. Because she was isolated and had no friends, there was no one to talk to about her escalating behavior. So we argued – constantly.

By age 16, I was pregnant and hiding it. When summer came I returned to my dad and step-mom and finally told.

My mom was devastated and cried for over an hour on the phone when we told her. She felt I'd betrayed her and was a scandal she had to deal with alone. I stopped talking to her altogether.

I raised my son alone, occasionally asking for financial help from her based on the bonds she'd saved for my college education. I moved back to California, went on to college years later and found a new career. But my relationship with Mom remained hostile and fractious no matter how hard we each tried to change it. And I wanted a mom desperately – one who was older than me, more mature than me, more experienced than me – who loved me. She wasn't it.

I felt like I was gypped somehow! I was supposed to have a loving mother who saw me and accepted me for just who I was. Why did I have her??? I thought that if I just said or did the right thing, we'd click! She'd stop judging and raging. She didn't. Most of my life choices have led back to two motivations: trying to get her acknowledgment and approval – or trying to push her completely away so she'd just leave me alone – once and for all!! Neither choice worked. I often thought I was crazy and psychotic!

I began to study metaphysics, and met friends in a spiritual community who mirrored back to me greater possibilities – and that I wasn't crazy. I found a school that focused on Spiritual Psychology, and began to uncover some of the many stories I'd told myself over the years. I began to realize how – in these stories – I was always the problem – always wrong, not enough, not worthy, smart, capable...

One day my mom went too far. I was visiting her and she sent the police to my hotel. She received a wrong number and thought it was me calling for help. She was convinced I was being held hostage by someone, and went into that irrational spiral I've experienced so often. Only this time she involved the police, hotel security and me in her delusion.

I called the author of this book, who immediately recognized the pain behind the story. And when I said, "Mom's acted like this since I was little – it's just getting worse!"

She asked me, "Have you considered that your mother has a psychosis?"

Those words changed my life – because up until that moment I always thought my mom was rational! And it was so clear that she wasn't. I began a new journey of discovery: How do I respond if I'm dealing with an irrational person who has no power, no dominion over me? How do I choose to love without letting in her venom and general hatred for everyone? If she's ill, how do I deal with her? Am I willing to mother myself?

Today, I have a spiritual foundation that has under-girded me and supported me in growing away from mere reactions. No more secrets. Today I've found a way to "interrupt the pattern" of taking in the accusatory, negative things she said until I'd become calm and clear about what was triggering me.

I've found the courage to say, "Do not speak to me that way. If you do, we won't talk anymore." Now she respects that. We're finding our way. It won't ever look like the loving 'ideal' I wanted, but it's as good as it can get. For me, that's enough. And I keep growing in my loving – trusting that the love will heal!

# Week Four
# Day One

## SURRENDERING SECRETS

Do you remember saying you never want to be like your mother or father—especially the aspects of them that consistently withheld information from family and each other?

Today, do you find yourself repeating certain patterns that seem familiar? Have you discovered family secrets and not understood why everyone held on so dearly to those old skeletons? Have you noticed you have done things you've been ashamed of, no matter how long ago they happened? Have you made a conscious or unconscious decision to keep these secrets buried deep inside? Have you gone through a trauma at someone else's hand and currently find yourself not wanting to share it because you do not want others to think badly of **you**?

**SECRETS** create emotional and physical blocks. **SECRETS** take an enormous amount of energy to hold, energy that could be used in constructive ways. **SECRETS** hold you hostage.

This week will be devoted to identifying secrets and releasing them. You do not have to share the secrets with anyone else. This exercise is just for you to get them out! Acknowledge them! Surrender them!

MEDITATION: (CD Track #5)

1. Put on some music (without lyrics) you really love or use the CD track on surrendering secrets.

2. Stand in the middle of the floor and close your eyes.

3. Breathe in and allow the music to comfort you.

4. Slowly allow your body to move to the music. The movements do not have to be big. As you feel more comfortable, use your hands to throw off any energy that feels restrictive. Actually move your hand down your arm, take the energy and throw it into the ground.

5. Repeat this with your head, shoulders, neck, hips, and thighs.

6. There is no right way to do this. Your body will tell you which areas are locked. Use this as a freedom dance and throw off energy. When you feel complete, sit down and write the experience in your journal.

7. Make sure you include any times you felt resistant or silly. All feelings and reactions are perfect for this process.

Ask yourself the following questions:

❖ How does it feel to release this energy?

❖ What shifts in my body occurred as I threw off the pain and hurt?

❖ What does this tell me about the energy I carry in my body?

❖ Are there any other areas in my body that need to be unlocked?

When the writing is complete, say the following affirmation:

*"I open my entire being to freedom. I call forward anything unlike the truth of my perfection, knowing nothing stands in the way of love revealing itself as my life now."*

Each day this week, meditate on your secrets. You will make a "SECRETS LIST." Write down anything that comes to mind on a piece of paper (not in your journal); especially those areas making you feel ashamed or uncomfortable. Even if it doesn't make sense or you already feel healed in this area add them to the list.

Add to the list every day.

## Day Two

# FEAR NOT

There is nothing to fear in God. The past is dead and the future does not exist. I have only now and so I bless this day. I am so grateful to have the opportunity to move forward and claim my destiny.

I honor the doubts that may arise within me. I recognize I am in control of my actions and reactions.

**AFFIRMATION:**

*"This is the day the Lord has made and I rejoice in it! Fear has no power over me now or ever!"*

## Day Three

# FACING MYSELF

This is the perfect time to stand strong in my resolve. I look at myself in the mirror and declare my independence. I recognize the beauty that God sees in me and I bask in a place of peace.

Truly, God's love is reflected back to me in everyone I meet.

**AFFIRMATION:**

*"I step out today as a free Spirit, expressing my lightness of being and having it returned to me one hundred fold."*

## Day Four

# ACKNOWLEDGING STRENGTH

Today, I give thanks for my perseverance. I applaud my willingness to step out and I dare to clean my **emotional house**. I am strong, clear, and brave.

My intention is strong and I am unwavering.

**AFFIRMATION:**

*"I am fearless! I am strong! I am powerful. There is an endless supply of comfort alive within me.*

## Day Five

# SURRENDER THE SHAME

There is no shame in me. God does not judge me. I take this opportunity to surrender judgments of myself and judgments of others. I have never done anything that deserves punishment.

God sees the truth of who I am right here and now. I can trust that the past has no control of my life. I have the power of choice and I exercise it here and now.

**AFFIRMATION:**

*"I embrace the divinity that is expressing as my life now. I let go of judgments and embrace self-love!"*

## Day Six

# BLAME NOT

I choose to shift my attention. I am clear that "judge not lest ye be judged" is an important statement to remember. I let go and let God handle the behavior of others. I choose peace!

I set an intention to move on and release the pain of the past. Clearly I am being blessed in this moment and I know it on every level.

**AFFIRMATION:**

*"I live a life of serenity and peace. I bless everyone who enters my thoughts. I want for others that which I want for myself."*

## Day Seven

# TAKING ACTION #4

I want to take this moment to honor your precious soul. You have come a long way and this week might have been quite challenging. You hung in there and that is a major accomplishment. Bravo!

**Put on some comforting music and sit down. Breathe in and relax your body. Allow this time to be just for you, a time when you rest in the gratitude of moving through this week. Acknowledge the wins, doubts, fears, tears, frustrations, and revelations. Take the time to process the week.**

**Now take out a piece of paper (not in your journal). You are going to write a letter to God. This letter will include all of the items from your SECRET LIST— those things you have been ashamed of in your life. PLEASE tell it all. Include any feelings that arise and do not censor. If tears come forward, take a moment to breathe, and continue to write. Once you are complete (this could take quite a bit of time), say a prayer of surrender and release.**

Burn the letter and the secret list as a symbol of letting go of the energy attached to the SECRETS.

### This is an important step.
### You do not want to hold onto this energy!

When you are finished say the following affirmation.

*"The power of sweet and total surrender engulfs me now.
I rest in the loving presence of Pure Spirit and all is well!"*

Now do something wonderful and nurturing for yourself. Take a bath, watch the sunset, take a walk or go to dinner at your favorite restaurant. The important thing is to take time to acknowledge your win. It is wonderful and worthy of celebration.

# Week Five
# Time For
# Forgiveness

*"Forgiveness is the exercise of compassion and is both a process and an attitude. In the process of forgiveness, we convert the suffering created by our own mistakes or as a result of being hurt by others into psychological and spiritual growth. Through the attitude of forgiveness, we attain happiness and serenity by letting go of the ego's incessant need to judge ourselves and others."*

~Joan Borysenko, **Guilt is the Teacher, Love is the Lesson** *(page 174)*

I used to think forgiveness was a magnanimous act. I was magnaimous when I could forgive someone who mistreated or acted inappropriate with me.

I used to believe forgiveness meant standing in a "holier than thou" place and deciding to bless someone for his or her transgressions.

How arrogant to think I had the power to forgive. I began researching, reading, and praying about the real meaning of forgiveness. I wanted to understand forgiveness beyond some 'ego need' motivating my actions. A graduate program in spiritual psychology provided the opportunity to study forgiveness. It was a rude awakening to discover that forgiveness isn't really necessary from Spirit or God's point of view. Where God is concerned, there is only energy, event, and circumstance. There is only possibility—no right or wrong.

## Forgiveness is a human concept.
___

Our perceptions and our judgments of any situation, event, or behavior of another being create our responses.

My mind exploded with this thought and I said to myself, "Wow! If that is really the case, then everything is about me and my concepts, my judgments, and perceptions." It meant forgiveness work was within me. It was not about condoning someone else's behavior. It was not about letting somebody off the hook. It was not about blessing someone and letting it go. It was about my personal filters and how I thought about this act or behavior, how I looked at the issue. It was the discovery of the filters through which I viewed everything.

I had another great revelation: I judged others in the same ways I judged myself. I had been unkind, unconscious, and violent with myself. That was a hard fact to swallow, since I wanted to be loving with myself and others. I needed to forgive myself for the judgments that were eating me alive.

Most of the people had moved on from these circumstances —I was the one still holding on. I was so locked into the judgments, I was in personal prison. The biggest challenge was getting past the rage about my stepfather's abuse. I still acted inappropriately and out of control in many moments.

In the book *Forgiveness: How To Make Peace With Your Past and Get On With Your Life*, Dr. Sidney B. Simon and Suzanne Simon wrote that forgiveness is something you do for yourself. Forgiveness is "working through the unfinished business, letting go of the pain, and moving on for your sake." (p.20)

The anger, rage, and judgments around my stepfather's acts kept us connected. For *my* peace of mind, I had to let go, so we could both be set free. It was an astounding revelation: I was responsible for holding him in my life. It became clear that I had to deepen my prayer work and open to my inner guidance.

His behavior was appalling and I would not wish it on any child. However, if I wanted to be free, I had to stop judging him as bad. I had to stop judging myself as wrong or unworthy. I had to find the place in my own life where I repeated the patterns of things he did to me. Where was I being abusive in my behavior to myself and others? Where wasn't I taking care of myself? Where was I abandoning myself?

The next step was to begin to forgive myself for the judgments. I had to start by proclaiming the truth of my life.

**I am a divine being
and a part of me
at the soul level
has never been harmed.**

There is a place within me that is whole and indestructible. In my divinity, I am one with the perfection and universal power of Spirit.

This huge awakening allowed me to begin to love myself. By daring to let go of the judgments and perceptions hardening my heart, I accepted the possibility of experiencing safety in my life.

This is an invitation for you to explore the same possibility, to let go of the judgments keeping you a prisoner of your past. We all have the power to let go, to release old perceptions, and live a power-filled, loving life.

## BILL'S STORY – AGE 51

Several years ago a friend of mine introduced me to an idea for a creative project. We became clear that it was something I felt inspired to produce with some involvement on his part. He was to serve as one of the many subjects offering creative input and we figured that his level of respect and influence would help to sell the project. I was to offer my creative visual talents, interview the subjects and piece it all together. I was under the impression that we were partners yet, nothing had yet been written into a formal contract. I placed my heart and soul into the project along with a great deal of my time and took advice from my friend along the way.

As the project gained momentum, we knew it was time to shop it around for a buyer. I brought in an agent who was interested in representing the project. Through the course of time and several phone conversations that I was not privy to, both my friend and our agent deemed it wiser for the two of them to pitch the project without me. I was informed that they planned on presenting the project in a way that centered around my friend, as his project with my creative assistance. Immediately upon hearing this, I felt stunned, as if I were in shock. Every part of me that had ever felt betrayed, left out or not seen was fully engaged. I spoke with them both and shared my thoughts and feelings, but from a "professional" point of view, the agent stuck with her conviction and my friend agreed with her. The project never found a buyer and for many years I held onto deep resentment, especially toward my friend. Every time I thought of him, I felt hurt and angry, and held deep judgments about his lack of care and respect for me and for others.

My body and emotions constricted and I felt the need to defend my position and make him wrong. Over the course of time, I realized that I didn't want to continue harboring these feelings for I knew that they would only hold me back from experiencing true freedom. I learned that as I held onto resentment and judgment, they continued to live inside of me and foster like a cancer. The bottom line was that I wanted to feel good about myself and not allow someone else's actions to effect me in this way.

I was given a series of techniques and tools for releasing all judgments attached to this situation and to arrive at a place of forgiveness. I made a commitment over the course of a four month period to practice these traits unwaveringly. I placed a photograph of my friend in my office and I would daily spend a moment taking time to send him love and to see his loving essence, who he really is. Three days a week I verbally practiced releasing all judgments I held toward my friend, the situation and toward myself, allowing forgiveness to be present.

Once a month I sent my friend a greeting card, checking in and sending love. I chose not to see him during this four month period, or for some time afterward. I knew that I needed the distance to not trigger into old patterns and wounds. At the end of the four months, I can honestly say that all of the emotional energy that had previously been present had left. Now, when I thought of him, all I saw was the loving being that was at his core. I knew that he was truly doing the best he knew how at that time and was working through his own life lessons.

I knew that I was not a victim in this scenario and I did the best I knew how at the time to be clear, strong and authentic. There was truly no 'charge' left in relation to my friend, the agent or myself. I felt at peace within myself and knew that there was never anything wrong with me, or the entire situation.

Years later, when I had no need whatsoever for any amends, my friend apologized from an open and loving heart.

## Week Five
## Day One

# FORGIVENESS = FREEDOM

Many people think of forgiveness as exoneration for someone else. Have you ever thought: Forgiveness is a sign of weakness. Why should I forgive after what he or she did to me? If I forgive, it will make them think it's okay. He doesn't deserve my forgiveness.

**Please be open to the following concept.** Your feelings and thoughts about this person are your perceptions or, more importantly, your judgments. Your unwillingness to forgive is hurting you, not them. Holding onto judgments keeps you imprisoned in a world of fear and condemnation.

Each time you judge someone, you are judging a part of yourself. Ask yourself:

❖ "Do I abuse, dishonor, or mistreat myself in anyway?"

❖ "Do I constantly dishonor my commitments to myself and others?"

❖ "Do I attack my body with unhealthy foods or refuse to honor my need for rest?"

❖ "Do I give the respect to others that I want for myself?"

❖ "Do I see myself as more important or above anyone else?"

If you answered yes to any one of these questions, you might consider putting down the stones of judgments you've been throwing.

During the next few days you will explore your relationship to judgments. I encourage you to be in the mode of the observer as you move through the week. **Do not use this week as another way to judge yourself.** Each of us has a powerful inner critic that loves to show us the bad or wrong things. I invite you to ask the critic to be still during this week to enable you to witness with a clear mind. This is a step toward becoming more conscious and freeing your amazing soul.

## MEDITATION: (CD Track #6)

**Allow the breath to move you to a state of relaxation. With each inhalation, breathe in the word "peace." With each exhalation, breathe out the word "judgment." Each exhalation will be a gentle reminder that you are letting go of judgment. Now, imagine you are in a beautiful place in nature. This place feels serene and calm. You could have been there before or it could be a new place.**

**Take in the beauty of the spot and feel the comfort and nurturing qualities this place offers. When you feel ready, open your eyes and pick up a piece of paper (not your journal). Make a list of people and situations that are challenging to you. The people may be dead or alive. The situation may be past or present, but if you still get upset when you think or speak about this person or situation, put it/them on the list. Do nothing but make the list.**

Ask the following questions to support the process:

❖ Is there any other judgment or fear wanting to be healed?

❖ Where are judgments still living within me?

❖ What relationships feel incomplete?

❖ What events still make me feel uncomfortable when I think of them?

❖ Is there anything or anyone else who needs to be on this list?

When you finish the list, say a prayer asking for clarity and peace where this list is concerned. When you are complete, say the following affirmation:

*"God's life is my life now. I stand in a place of readiness to embrace the peace that passes all human understanding."*

More people, situations, or memories may emerge during the week. Add them to the list.

# Day Two

# EXPLORATION

I am open to discovering the places within me that have felt hurt and wounded. This is clearly an act of courage and a leap of faith. I know the Universe is supporting me every step of the way.

I dare to step into any dark or shadow space living within me because God is there.

**AFFIRMATION:**

*"I am not alone! God is always with me and I can trust that above all else!"*

### Day Three

# FEEL THE FEELINGS

Feelings that emerge are not my enemies. I choose to look at them as steps to my freedom. The memories coming forward are at my request, to facilitate my healing.

I am not afraid to feel.

**AFFIRMATION:**

*"Today, I draw comfort in knowing I cannot fail in God. Love surrounds me in each moment. I am at peace!"*

# Day Four

# VULNERABILITY

How good it is to know that vulnerability is not a weakness. How comforting to know this exploration assists me in revealing the truth and beauty of my soul.

I give thanks for being guided every step of the way and nothing can stop me now. All new feelings and memories are opportunities for me to move past my fears and "fly high" in Spirit.

**AFFIRMATION:**

*"I radiate divine love in each moment. I am clear that miracles are unfolding in my life now!"*

## Day Five

# FLOOD GATES ARE OPEN

Today, I stand strong in knowing God is right where I am. I allow each moment to be a learning experience. I am recognizing my need to reveal all that has been locked inside for so long.

I place my attention on relaxing and letting go. I know I am held in the light of the Holy Spirit.

**AFFIRMATION:**

*"I stand in gratitude as I open to the fullness of my experience. I embrace my divinity in every area of my life!"*

## Day Six

# GENTLE WITH MYSELF

I take this day to focus on loving myself. I create opportunities to nurture myself and acknowledge my dedication to this process of healing.

I deserve to be pampered and I give this gift of compassion to myself in joyous ways.

**AFFIRMATION:**

*"The gift of love is present as I move through this day. I gently allow myself to rest and rejuvenate."*

## Day Seven

# TAKING ACTION # 5

You are an amazing person and you should be very proud of yourself. The love you have shown yourself this week by empowering your steps to freedom is magnificent. I enthusiastically recognize you!

**As you moved through this week, many feelings and thoughts may have surfaced. Go back to your paper and review the list that began the week, including what you have added. Look carefully at the prevailing judgments. Now sit in a comfortable place. Recognizing each judgment of another or of yourself, begin the following process. Place your hand over your heart. State the following:**

**I stand as a space of forgiveness.**

**I am surrendering the blame of _____ and of myself.**

**I am surrendering judgments of _____ and of myself.**

**I am releasing the guilt and shame attached to this event.**

**Example:** I surrender the blame of Mary as abusive and unkind. I surrender the blame of myself for any acts of abusive or unkind behavior. I surrender the judgments of

Mary as selfish and controlling. I surrender the judgments of myself as selfish and controlling. I release the guilt and shame attached to this event. I recognize that Mary was doing the best she could in that moment. I recognize that I have always done the best that I could and I am a loving and kind person. I take this moment to honor myself. Now repeat these words.

**I CHOOSE:**
**To release self-condemnation**
**To release shame**
**To release blame**
**To release guilt**
**To release unkind thoughts**
**To release belief in my unworthiness**

**You do not have to feel any particular way. You are not being required to totally let go of your feelings. This is a process. You are simply using the power of your word to release the energy of judgment locked in your consciousness. When you are complete with the list, go into prayer. Visualize giving the list to God and give thanks for the opportunity to move beyond the judgments.**

**Burn the List.**

# WEEK SIX
# RECLAIMING YOURSELF

*"Can you be like a newborn child? The baby cries all day and yet his voice never becomes hoarse. That is because he has not lost nature's harmony. At the core of our being this eternal child exists, truly alive, awaiting embodiment in our actions and our attitudes. And the light of the world can shine through it."*
~*Various Contributors,* **Reclaiming The Inner Child** *(p. 5)*

Let's take a moment to discuss freedom in more depth. Freedom is not walking away from everything and having no responsibilities. It's not being wealthy enough to buy anything you want. It's not declaring you are free, yet making choices that bind you to old behaviors no longer serving you.

## Freedom is knowing you are a spiritual being connected to a Universal Source.

Quantum physics says there is a quantum domain where an unending energy is ever evolving. We are a part of that domain and there is a field of pure potential available to us. All we have to do is align ourselves with the ever-present and always abundant energy.

Standing in the space of freedom means you are willing to remember:

❖ You are always connected and Spirit is your Source.

❖ Every moment, right here and right now, is a choice point.

❖ You get to choose how you live, speak, walk, etc.

Don't be fooled into thinking you are not making choices. Everything is a choice. If you are choosing to be in abusive relationships, it's a choice. If you are opening to unharmonious, non-nurturing, and unsupportive careers or jobs, it's a choice. If you are living in a place of health, mental well being and financial abundance, that also is a choice. Make no mistake about it.

If you have come from unsupportive environments, families, and relationships or have been traumatized or abused, it is difficult to be clear. It is harder to see where the lines of choice fall. What you can do is make choices from the point of view... little things first.

❖ Today I choose to take care of myself

❖ Today I choose to be loving with myself

❖ Today I choose to do something physical to open up the channels of my body

❖ Today I choose to pray and remember my connection to God

Little steps create vast pathways of self-realization. These little steps are the ways we reclaim our true selves. You begin to attract what you put into the universe. When you decide to be healthy, when you decide to be open, when you decide to be connected to strong, loving people, a powerful energy goes into the universe and becomes a magnet. There is a quote, *"love brings up anything unlike itself,"* meaning when you fall in love, there is beautiful bliss and anything not supporting love surfaces to be healed and transformed.

The same is true of intention. If you decide to be on the path of freedom, your mind brings up anything into your conscious awareness that doesn't support you being free. It can look like any number of things. It may look like fear, anxiety, or the certainty that things are falling apart. If it happens, don't panic and decide changing isn't worthwhile. It is in these moments you say, "Ah! It's time for me to move into the role of witness versus judge. Witness what is happening in my life and choose, moment by moment, what I am going to do to support myself to fully stand in freedom. This time I choose to fully express and open to the infinite possibilities awaiting me."

I invite you in this moment to take a gentle look at your freedom. Are you free? Are you open? Are you available? Are you willing to stand in the face of fear and claim who you are? Are you willing to use your gifts? Are you willing to allow any locked places within you to have a voice? Are you willing to reclaim yourself and step out in bold ways as a declaration of your greatness? I say, activate the YES! It lives in your soul and is waiting to be released to support you in soaring to a greater life. I say....**DO IT NOW!**

## THOM'S STORY – AGE 42

I am honored to add my story to a book that, I know, will be a powerful source of healing and support for so many people. I thank you for the opportunity to play a small part in this important work.

I experienced sexual abuse from age seven to age thirteen. It was shrouded in love, and I was told to feel lucky. I was under the constant threat of physical abuse from my earliest memories. I can't remember too many days that didn't include yelling and fighting in my house. On one occasion, I watched my sister as she was dragged across the kitchen floor, listened as her scalp popped loose from her skull and witnessed her being beaten with a fly swatter until it broke in my mother's hand. I knew that if I wasn't "good" that I could be next. My child's mind needed to find a way to be perfect so I could feel safe. Everyone knew that my mother beat my sister because it was impossible to hide. I thought I was the lucky one. But, I didn't know that the "love" I was receiving in private would leave scars just as deep.

For so long I believed that I couldn't be **'normal'** because my childhood was not normal. I grew up feeling very **alone** because I assumed that my home life was different from my school friends. I felt **powerless** because many in authority over me **abused** my trust and took my power. I didn't feel like a real person because I was treated like an **object** or a possession. In a house where **alcohol** was the drug of choice, where **violence** and the threat of violence were constant and where **love was painfully distorted**, I survived.

The pain of child abuse is complicated. It's not a clean wound. Different experiences changed me in different ways. Through violence I was taught not to question authority and to give away my control. Because I had no control over my life I didn't know how to set healthy boundaries. This left me open to abuse from outside my family. I didn't know what healthy expressions of anger looked like. I chose not to express anger at all, until it boiled over.

Looking at my history it's amazing that I am now a husband and father. My faith has always guided my journey and supported my highest priorities. There were many years when I was convinced that I would never have this life. I was not optimistic that I would ever find a relationship but I knew I could put my energy into friendships, my career and service to the world. I studied the words of Jesus, Gandhi, Martin Luther King and Mother Teresa and found that through their example I could deepen my faith in my higher power and journey through my challenges. Through my faith path, counseling and a drive to get to the core of my issues, I began a quest for my authentic power. I began the journey of facing my fears and looking into the dark rooms that I had kept shut inside me for so many years. Even after I was married, I wouldn't think of having children until I faced those fears as well. There were two roads that I could foresee and a third I could only dream of; 1) I would continue the cycle of abuse or 2) I would keep my distance and never be comfortable around my kids for fear of hurting them in some way or 3) have a loving, happy, healthy, and close relationship to my kids. I have found that amazing relationship with my children, my wife and myself.

Practical spirituality has taught me that I am a product of my total journey. I am a product of both my past experiences and my conscious focus to move beyond my past experiences. I have stopped looking for a destination. I am in **love** with the journey! I wake up everyday knowing that I am now in control of my life and my future. My past exists inside me everyday, but the pain has been replaced with a calm confidence in who I have become. I am a child advocate and a supporter for parent education now. I teach children how to connect with one another and how to see that our similarities far outweigh our differences. I love my life and all that is in my life; therefore I am grateful for every experience that has brought me to this place. I am an instrument of peace in my world and I owe it all to my total journey. When I look at the scope of where I came from to where I am I can never doubt the existence of limitless possibilities in all of our lives. Stay honest and vulnerable, trust in the journey and keep taking steps toward that peaceful, loving place where we all belong. Together we will change the world.

# Week Six
# Day One

# CHANGE

Have you thought about what **you** want? What **you** need? What will ignite you and propel you into your divine plan? Do you feel confused or unsure about what you want to do now? **This is a good thing!!** It means you are ready to create. You are ready to paint the canvas of your life in ways not imagined before. All that has been stripped away allows you the opportunity to begin again.

## You are ready to accept that you are a Masterpiece of the Divine!

Each day this week will be devoted to assisting you in declaring your magnificence. I encourage you to step beyond all limiting thoughts and beliefs. Dare to dream BIG!

**MEDITATION: (CD Track #7)**

Sit down and close your eyes. Begin to breathe. Allow yourself to get comfortable and relaxed. Imagine you have all the money you will ever need. See yourself on a dream vacation, relaxed, peaceful and joyous. Think about what you would like to do with the rest of your life. Remember you have all the money you will ever need. Allow your mind to go anywhere it wants to go. There are no limits. You can do whatever you like. Nothing is silly or out of reach. Where would you be in one year? Five years? Fifteen years?

Use these questions to assist you:

❖ How would I be operating in the world without limitation?

❖ What kind of friends would I have?

❖ Where would I live?

❖ What kind of relationships would be in my life?

❖ What would I do if I were wealthy?

When you feel complete, open your eyes and write in your journal. Include all the thoughts that came to your mind. Please don't edit, because your rational mind says it's impossible. Now say the following affirmation:

*"My life is rich and full of amazing treasures. I live my dream. I embrace God's vision for my life now!"*

If more thoughts or ideas arise this week adding to your vision, feel free to write them in your journal.

## Day Two

# COMPLETIONS

Today I make a list of all the things that are not complete in my life. Things I have started and never finished. Calls never made. Bills needing to be paid. Closets to be cleaned. Letters to be written. An apology I have been putting off.

It is time to begin to clean house on all levels and I am ready.

**AFFIRMATION:**

*"There is nothing standing in the way of my freedom except me. I affirm my willingness to bask in the joy of my life!"*

## Day Three

# PRIORITIES

I list, in order of priority, the items on my completion list. I set a firm intention to move through each item with ease and grace. I give myself a time limit and I begin to see the light at the end of the tunnel.

Each action moves me closer to expressing my divine plan.

**AFFIRMATION:**

*"Peace fills my soul as I face and embrace my responsibilities. I ask for God's assistance as I move forward. Life is Good!"*

## Day Four

# LIGHT MY FIRE

I am excited as I make a list of all the things that bring me joy. I allow the child within me to express fully. The dreams and desires flood forth with amazing ease.

I am ignited at the thought of exploring the items on this list. My heart smiles.

**AFFIRMATION:**

*"I leap into new areas of awareness! The desires of my heart are blossoming in this moment and I radiate ecstasy!*

## Day Five

# QUALITES OF GOD

I choose one or two qualities of God expressing my dedication to myself and my life. I make sure I feel open and expansive when I say the word(s) out loud.

Today, I recognize who I am and I share myself and my gifts.

**AFFIRMATION:**

*"God's life is my life now. I am light and love and I rejoice!"*

## Day Six

# AFFIRMING THE TRUTH

I create an affirmation using the quality(s) of God that came forward yesterday. I choose words that are empowering and inspiring to me each time I see them.

I ask Spirit to assist me in proclaiming my power.

**AFFIRMATION:** *(put your affirmation here)*

*"I am*

_____

_____

_____

_____

_____

*"*

## Day Seven

# TAKING ACTION #6

Incredible! That's what you are. How wonderful that you took the time this week to stand in your power and take action. Fabulous work!

**Today is dedicated to creativity and intention merging. Take out your list of completions, list of priorities, joy list, quality(s) of God, and your affirmation. Get some construction paper (pick a color that ignites you), crayons, watercolors, and colorful stickers. You can make one large collage, but I encourage you to make one for each list. Take the list from each day and make it a work of art. Make each as beautiful as you possibly can, something you would want to frame or laminate. There are no restrictions. Place them in your office, on your altar, or someplace often seen. These will be reminders of your freedom and success. In fact, they will be visual affirmations of a reclaimed and re-mastered you.**

**I have included a couple of my creativity projects to give you an idea of how it can look.**

**When you are complete, say your affirmation, put on some music, dance, and take a bow!**

# Week Seven
# Radical
# Self Care

*"Our mental and emotional diets determine our overall energy levels, health, and well-being to a far greater extent than most people realize. Every thought and feeling, no matter how big or small, impacts our inner energy reserves."*
~Doc Childre and Howard Martin, **The HeartMath Solution**

I sat in a meeting where people shared what they wanted to do with their lives and identified the focus of their attention. One woman said, "Well, I'm putting my attention on radical self-care."

I looked at her and thought, "Wow, that has been my journey over the last several years; learning how to take care of myself, learning how to self-nurture and how to have balance in my life." I remembered taking a class about self-nurturing. When the assignment was given, I wondered, "Do I know how to do that?" I know how to take care of other people. I know how to work hard and take care of my job and my colleagues. But, I'm not sure I know how to take care of myself. The entire class revealed a glimpse of what it would be like to take care of myself. **It was a course in Radical Self-Care... meaning that 'I' come first.**

This is an interesting concept because when you have been a caretaker and placed other needs beyond your own, there appears to be no other options. Your first reaction in thinking about radical self-care could be the fear that people are going to be upset or annoyed. There will be some sort of resistance because you have *always* been the one to handle things. You're probably right. You will be asking people to adapt to a new way of operating *with you*. They won't understand and will use creative methods to bring you back to the caretaker role. It will be easy to say okay and slip back into the old pattern of doing for others rather than doing for yourself.

*Here is the good news.*

## I have discovered over the last several years that the more I take care of myself, the more time and compassion is available for others.

Today, my interaction with other people and the interaction with my career are from a healthy standpoint rather than from need—need to be validated, need to be in control, need to feel important, need to be loved.

You have the chance to learn how to take care of yourself. You can discover what nurtures you. For me, it's hot baths with candles, walks, meditation, and reading great books that feed my soul. It's turning on music and dancing around the house. It makes me feel joyous and alive.

Take time to determine what you need to feel cared for and comforted. Begin by building an intentionally nurturing schedule. If you can't start daily, try weekly. What are you willing to do once a week to nurture yourself? What are you willing to do to feel better, healthier, more conscious and balanced? Once you have made the choice, make that time sacred, without interruption. It may be uncomfortable at first. It will feel like you are in a void or in limbo because it's foreign. Do it anyway, for you will discover a place of health and balance that opens portals for new and exciting possibilities in your life.

## MONIQUE'S STORY - AGE 38

Life is filled with revelations, small and large. There is not a day that goes by that I don't discover something new and exciting about my self and the world. When I was a girl I saw my life unfolding as the perfect fairy tale that included prince charming, a castle and the horse he road in on. Like most little girls believed, "I'll have this all by age twenty-five." By the time I turned twenty-five and there were no castles, horses, knights in shining armor or ball gowns, I knew I had to figure something out. I hadn't planned my life beyond the big day and riding off into the sunset.

Taking responsibility for myself was and continues to be a huge revelation. I had spent my entire life waiting for someone to come and rescue me since I was three. And there is nothing more life transforming than realizing no one is coming- I'm it! This idea that someone would surely rescue me was depleting my life of everything worthy, creative, and necessary I had to offer. It kept my attention focused outward, expecting someone else's gifts, power and strength. Never once did I turn inward for the answers to my own happiness, purpose or success. Never at all did I consider what I have to offer. For years, I overlooked my greatest and only asset – me.

This behavior reared it head in every thread of my life and consciousness. I didn't believe in myself which means I had no idea who I was. I found that I was often insecure and uncertain around people who were empowered. I relied on the expertise of others for my emotional health and well-being. And I often decided how to feel about myself based upon responses I received from others.

Soon I began seeing the cost of adjusting my attitude or feelings according to the consensus. I was in a relationship with a young man who had a dominant personality. I witnessed within a few months his ideas had become my ideas. On the surface this was no big deal, but inwardly I was relinquishing beliefs and concepts that had been life sustaining, for his comfort. This was the revelation that showed me I had not been living my life while waiting for someone to live it for me.

Today I'm married to the young man with the dominant personality, and our relationship has a way of strengthening me while softening him and vice versa. This is due to my deep intention to be the person I was created to be and show up for myself courageously. This requires a depth of self-love, adoration and acceptance I had not known before I was thirty. Continuously I'm at my growing edge which brings me back to myself at three years old, waiting for someone to rescue me. I look her in the eyes extend my arms; embracing her, I whisper… I'm it.

## Week Seven
## Day One

# READY, SET, GO!

Well, it's the last week. How do you feel? Please take this moment to honor yourself. You have shown courage and strength, and you deserve to be acknowledged.

**MEDITATION: (CD Track #8)**

Go to your quiet place and become still. Close your eyes, breathe, and take some time to relax. Think about all the work (inner and outer) you have done over the past few weeks. Give thanks for all the things you have learned and experienced. When you feel complete, say your affirmation.

Now, take out the story you wrote on the first day. Take a moment to give thanks for the story that brought you to this point, bless it and **BURN IT**. It is no longer the truth of your life.

Take out your journal and write your new story. Include all the wonderful things you will accomplish since money is no object. Include all of your dreams and desires. Share the truth of your loving relationships and the profound difference you make on the planet.

The following questions might help:

❖ What destiny is calling me forward?

❖ What is the highest vision for my life?

❖ What adventures await me now that I am free?

❖ How will grace and ease guide my path to a new life?

❖ How will love reveal itself to me now?

When you are complete, hold the story next to your heart and close your eyes. Allow yourself to really "drink" in the power of your new story.

## Day Two

## SELF-ACCEPTANCE

I am so thankful for who I am and the difference I make in people's lives. Right where I am is perfect and there is nothing to do but stand in gratitude.

I am a blessing and a gift.

**AFFIRMATION:** *(put your affirmation here)*

_____

_____

_____

_____

_____

# Day Three

# SELF-COMPASSION

I am gentle with myself and others. When I want to judge someone, I ask myself if I possess that quality or exhibit that behavior. I take a moment to send out a blessing.

I send love and compassion to everyone I meet and in turn I experience it ten-fold.

**AFFIRMATION:** *(put your affirmation here)*

_____

_____

_____

_____

_____

## Day Four

# SELF-TRUST

I trust God. I trust love. I trust myself. I walk by grace and I face this day knowing that everything is working for my highest and best.

My faith is strong and guides my every move. Miracles unfold before my very eyes.

**AFFIRMATION**: *(put your affirmation here)*

_____

_____

_____

_____

_____

## Day Five

# CREATIVE SELF-EXPRESSION

My creativity is boundless. I open to new ways of sharing my gifts in expansive and artistic ways. I take every opportunity in my life to be a chance to express my creativity in glorious ways.

I am clear that creativity permeates every area of my life. I am co-creating with God in every moment.

**AFFIRMATION:** *(put your affirmation here)*

_____

_____

_____

_____

_____

## Day Six

# DIVINE SELF-EXPRESSION

Spirit is guiding me and I can see the divine opportunities available to me in every moment. Gifts and infinite possibilities flow to me easily and effortlessly.

The doors to my destiny are open and I step through to fulfill my divine purpose.

**AFFIRMATION:** *(put your affirmation here)*

_____

_____

_____

_____

_____

## Day Seven

# TAKING ACTION #7

WOW! YOU DID IT! BRAVO!

Put on some beautiful music and sit down with your journal. Close your eyes and breathe in how wonderful it feels to have committed to and completed this process. Take as long as you like. This is a moment to really acknowledge your accomplishment.

When you are relaxed, open your eyes and take out your journal. Write a love letter to YOU from Spirit. This is the kind of letter you have always wanted to get. Honor your perseverance, kindness, loving nature, wonderful heart, and desire to grow. Make sure you sign it God or Spirit or Divine Intelligence. When you are complete, read it aloud. Whenever you feel that you might be stuck or unsure, I invite you to re-read this letter. It will have a strong impact.

# MOVING FORWARD

This seven-week program is a strong beginning to your greater unfolding. It is important you not stop here. I encourage you to say your personal affirmation daily and follow-through on your completions list. It will anchor your freedom and promote movement.

You have been given tools to assist in your freedom, but most people need more time to complete the exercises, deal with the re-emerging patterns, and face resistance that wants to keep us small. You will never go back to the beginning because now you have experienced a shift. Remember, the old patterns want to live. They will keep changing form to fool you into thinking they are gone. It's important to keep your spiritual channels open so you can recognize an old habit in a new form.

**Some of the ways to recognize a disguised habit are:**

❖ Return of negative self-talk

❖ Inability to speak authentically

❖ Diminished self-nurturing

❖ Telling the old story again

❖ Discontinuing your spiritual practice

❖ Eating foods that do not serve you

❖ Not exercising or supporting your body with movement

❖ Re-emergence of old anger patterns

❖ Doubting what you know supports you

❖ Surrendering your power to someone else

❖ Playing small to keep the peace

❖ Too busy to spend time with yourself

**Any or all of these are signs to STOP and go back to the basics.**

❖ Find quiet time to pray and meditate

❖ Journal your feelings

❖ Explore your body to see if it is constricted

❖ Move your body

❖ Give your feelings a voice

❖ Read your new story

❖ Say your personal affirmation or pick one from the book

❖ Use this book by opening to a page and reading the affirmation for the day

Connecting to the quietude of your soul is very important. Your mind will be able to fool you into irrational beliefs and reactions. But your inner voice, that "still-point" within you knows the power of love and compassion will never steer you wrong. It will be a constant source of guidance to bring you back to the remembrance of a healthy state of being.

# THOUGHTS
# ON MEDITATION

Meditation is an amazing gift. It allows us to slow down and connect with the invisible power of the Spirit or Universe. It moves us out of the realm of BETA state where we are concerned with the physical world. It allows us to activate the ALPHA state where we tap into the field of pure potential and spiritual oneness. It is the place where we can experience silence and begin to *hear* untapped information available to support our divinity.

If you have challenges meditating, here are a few tools to assist:

❖ Put on soft and soothing music.

❖ Start small. Five minutes is a great place to start.

❖ Invite love into the meditation and ask for assistance in discovering stillness.

❖ Pick a short affirmation to say each time your mind wanders or becomes overactive (I am open to Divine Guidance, I am healing now, The joy of God is my joy).

❖ Use your personal affirmation to bring you back to center.

❖ Pick a word and use it as a mantra (instrument of the mind). LOVE, PEACE, HARMONY, SURRENDER, HEALING.

❖ Ask a question for contemplation. Who am I? What is faith? What is love? What is joy? What is health?

❖ Use the breath. On the inhale, count in slowly to five and then on the exhale count back to one.

❖ Take a hike, sit in nature and become still.

❖ Let go of any expectations. If you continue to practice, you will find the perfect form of meditation.

Once you find the suitable formula for meditation, it will be a gift supporting you like no other. It can be used at home, in a park, in your office, in a restroom or when sitting in your car in a parking lot waiting for a meeting or event. It is one of the quickest ways to quiet the mind and experience internal peace.

# THOUGHTS ON PRAYER

It does not matter how you pray. It is important that you pray, find a way to connect and open to the in-dwelling Spirit that is your life. Some people use the Bible, some pray by chanting, some read prayers from ancient wisdom writings. **It is all good if it works for you.**

Some are challenged because their initial introduction to prayer did not work for them.

Below is a form of affirmative prayer. It is a tool that may assist you in learning to pray if it has been a challenge. You can express the following in your own words and in any way that feels supportive to your peace of mind.

RECOGNIZE that there is only one God. That this God is the energy of love, compassion, joy, harmony, and is all there is. It is in every religion, every culture, every walk of life. It is the essence of life itself.

State that you are UNIFIED with this energy. That it lives in you and through you. That the harmony and peace of God is accessible to you because you are connected.

REALIZE that the perfection of God is present and available in your life. Realize the Universe is conspiring to support your freedom and your unfolding destiny. Everything you need is available now.

Give THANKS for the answered prayer, for the love surrounding you, for the peace that passes all human understanding. Express gratitude for the many gifts unfolding for you today.

RELEASE the prayer. Let go and let God handle the details. There are Universal laws in place supporting the prayer in a grand and glorious fashion.

It has been my pleasure to guide you on this journey. You have all the resources within you that are necessary. God is always with you. Take time to be still, pray and listen. Your answers will come with ease and you will be guided to places you cannot imagine at this moment.

Enjoy your journey. Even the challenging times offer great insights and amazing gifts. Know that you are unique and came here to do great things. I know that about you and I hold you in my heart and in my prayers always.

Much love and light,

*Cynthia*

# MORE ABOUT

# CYNTHIA JAMES

To this point, you've only read a portion of the stories that make up this remarkable woman.

Cynthia is a lecturer, teacher and internationally renowned performing artist. She was the co-host of a talk show in Los Angeles. She has counseled thousands of people; in corporate environments, as one-on-one clients, couples and created youth programs. She's facilitated hundreds of workshops and seminars and has been a featured speaker in business and spiritual forums.

Her life has transformed as she transcended her childhood of violence and abuse. Through education and personal healing, Cynthia created the foundation for this program and many other classes that integrate traditional therapeutic techniques, music, creativity and spiritual processes.

Ms. James graduated from two Masters Degree programs, one in spiritual psychology and one in consciousness studies. She currently serves as an associate minister at Mile Hi Church, one of the largest new thought spiritual centers in the world, with a congregation of over 10,000 member and friends.

Cynthia lives and thrives in the mountains of Colorado with her husband Carl.

# CYNTHIA JAMES' MUSIC

### I Live For Thee
Music to Lift &
Inspire the Heart & Soul

available through CDBaby.com

### Transcendence
Vocals & Piano Uplifting Hearts

Piano: Kent Rautenstraus

available through CDBaby.com

### Standing in the Light
Music to Celebrate
Our Spiritual Connection

available through CDBaby.com

## Meditation Series

### Spirit of the Inner Child
### Finding Your Purpose
### Releasing Rage
### Transforming Memories

available through CDBaby.com

# CYNTHIA JAMES' WORKSHOPS

## What Will Set You Free
## Weekend Intensive

**Set yourself free and come into your power.**

Through this integrative experience, each participant is given the opportunity to explore old patterns and expand into new ways of being. This is a transformational workshop that creates a safe space to:

- ❖ Face beliefs that no longer serve you
- ❖ Release old fears
- ❖ Address emotional wounds
- ❖ Claim the full experience that is your life

**For information and dates of Cynthia's workshops, write to:
Cynthia@WhatWillSetYouFree.com**

# Sacred Woman, Holy Life

A creative and experiential adventure. This workshop is an exploration and discovery journey to uncover and fully express the true purpose for your life as a woman. You will learn how to:

❖ Embrace nature's relationship to the essence of women
❖ Deepen your spiritual practice
❖ Explore rituals and movements
❖ Enjoy music and creative expression

# Revealing Your Authentic Image
## co-facilitated with world renowned photographer Carl Studna, MA

This is an experiential workshop utilizing video, still photography, Science of Mind and Spirit principles that teaches you how to release the "true essence of you" on film.

# ORDER FORM
## What Will Set You Free
## Book & CD Set

## $19.95 + 2.50 (S&H)

online at:
http://www.WhatWillSetYouFree.com

by phone:
have your credit card handy and call:
(303) 794-8888

by fax:
(720) 863-2013

by mail:
send check payable to:
Thornton Publishing, Inc.
17011 Lincoln Ave. #408
Parker, Colorado 80134

If it is temporarily sold out at your favorite bookstore,
have them order more of ISBN: 0-9774761-8-9

Name: _____
Address: _____
_____
Phone: _____
E-mail: _____

Credit Card #: _____
Card Type: _____          Expiration Date: ____/ ____
Security Code: _____